The Vintage Home

The Vintage Home

CLEVER FINDS AND FADED TREASURES FOR TODAY'S CHIC LIVING

JUDITH WILSON

First published in 2008 by Jacqui Small LLP,
an imprint of Aurum Press, 7 Greenland Street, London NW1 0ND

ISBN: 978 1 906417 16 1

A catalogue record for this
book is available from
the British Library.

2010 2009 2008
10 9 8 7 6 5 4 3 2 1

Printed in China

PUBLISHER Jacqui Small
COMMISSIONING EDITOR Jo Copestick
MANAGING EDITOR Lesley Felce
DESIGNER Ashley Western
EDITOR Hilary Mandleberg
PRODUCTION Peter Colley
PICTURE RESEARCH Nadine Bazar

contents

There's an enduring appeal to the vintage home. At its heart lies a timeless classic style: a carefully evolved mix of gently aged furniture, retro textiles and quirky accessories, which can be dressed down to suit a country interior or given an edgy twist for a modern space. Yet the vintage look has also become the darling of the fashion and interiors world and yesterday's junk is now deemed desirable. While vintage designer furniture has achieved cult status (with prices to match), other vintage buys are inexpensive, so it can be a cost-effective choice. Even better, most retro pieces are already gently distressed, so there's no need to worry about another knock or dent.

Yet this new-found obsession with nostalgia, especially for 20th-century pieces, isn't just about perfecting a style. Perhaps, as we teeter on the edge of this new millennium, we feel comforted by surrounding ourselves with things from our childhood. Certainly, many of us have tired of mass-produced high-street merchandise and identikit modern interiors. Whatever the reason, all things 20th-century are a hot topic, and many dealers and specialist websites are now devoted to helping us source that perfect retro buy.

With its emphasis on saving and reusing, the vintage home is also perfectly in tune with today's eco conscience. It isn't new to value pieces from the past — whether for their excellent craftsmanship or beautiful patina. But giving an old piece a second life means fewer reasons to buy cheap new furniture and less rubbish cluttering up our landfill sites. Going vintage also means your home will be unique. Treasuring old things, with their inherent sense of history, imparts soul. Put together your vintage home with a tongue-in-cheek irreverence, and you'll have the perfect short-cut to a beautiful, personal and thrifty new home.

OPPOSITE: For an eclectic look, it's important to mix vintage buys with the occasional modern piece. In this French apartment, a distressed floor and painted panelling are combined with classic Charles and Ray Eames chairs and a contemporary table.

Choosing Vintage

Choosing vintage style can enhance any type of home. A smattering of well-worn pieces can bring a sense of connection to period architecture; a modern space will be softened by echoes of the past. And once you've accepted that some well-loved pieces may need careful handling and occasional running repairs, you can congratulate yourself that re-using is "green" and that foraging for finds is a gentle and enjoyable art.

OPPOSITE ABOVE LEFT A mix of styles and periods is fun. Here, original 60s wallpaper is combined with an Eero Saarinen table and chairs and a kitsch sunburst mirror.

OPPOSITE ABOVE RIGHT If you want a look from a particular decade, as in this 70s room, do your research to get the details right.

OPPOSITE CENTRE LEFT A varied mix of pieces needs one element to pull everything together. Here, a graphic 40s rug unifies everything from a neoclassical cabinet to a black lacquer table.

OPPOSITE CENTRE RIGHT The combination of a Charles and Ray Eames 20th-century chair and an antique battered metal cupboard provides a dramatic contrast.

OPPOSITE BELOW LEFT Magpie shoppers should choose a cohesive theme for display. Black and white works well in a small bathroom.

OPPOSITE BELOW RIGHT A worn patina can be part of a piece's allure. This Arne Jacobsen classic from the 50s is gently distressed but still beautiful.

As a style, the huge benefit of vintage is that it's easy to mix and achievable on a low budget. Unless you're looking for serious investment furniture, it's relatively easy to pick up whacky accessories without paying the earth. Hovering as it does between junk and serious antiques, vintage style doesn't have a blueprint, but a well-worn, casually thrown together mood certainly defines it. And vintage can be interpreted to suit: there's relaxed country vintage, glamorous boudoir vintage, sophisticated retro vintage and gritty urban vintage.

How you accumulate your vintage pieces is all down to your budget, time and inclination. Are you happy with pavement finds or do you want to save up for a quality designer piece? If you're a cash-rich, time-poor collector, there are vintage furniture specialists who can hunt out a special find for you. But if you're happy to while away your weekends checking out junk shops, vintage can be the start of a lifelong passion. Once you've started, it may be difficult to stop.

THIS PAGE Use a strong architectural feature as a springboard to inform your vintage choices. In this apartment, the scroll motifs of the iron staircase and the tall columns are balanced by the rounded shapes of several robust old leather armchairs.

WHY VINTAGE?

Anyone who's ever furnished a new home will know that it's both extremely expensive – as well as a little soulless – to start entirely from scratch. Most of us come with "baggage", whether that's some favourite furniture from a previous home or a few inherited accessories.

The beauty of vintage is that it thrives on such "baggage": it depends on a casually pulled-together, rich hotch-potch of styles, finishes and shapes. And precisely because much of the interest and drama derives from the pieces, vintage is also a brilliant option if you're not keen on highly decorated, fussy interiors. A simple background is best so the treasures can take centre-stage.

ARCHITECTURE

If your home has particularly dominant period architecture, this can be the inspiration for choosing retro pieces. A 20s home with smallish rooms and modest casement windows, for example, may cry out to be filled with mid-20th-century furniture that will suit its proportions. A converted city warehouse will look stunning filled with large-scale salvaged industrial fittings. A 70s home – once held in scorn by the movers and shakers of the interiors world – is the perfect repository for a nostalgic collection of 70s furniture and accessories.

But vintage isn't about faithfully furnishing a home to resemble its period original. Instead, use your architecture as an inspirational springboard, then hunt for pieces that suit the prevailing mood. Break rules and play with contrasts. Kitting out a contemporary city apartment or a pristinely painted period townhouse with distressed pieces, for instance, can look extraordinarily dramatic. And if your home's architecture is just plain boring, then placing the emphasis on a few great pieces can deflect attention from it.

The location and materials of your home can also offer the cue you need to guide a vintage theme. For example, a country home blessed with original old floorboards and unevenly plastered walls will look great with shabby-chic Victorian sofas and the bumpy weave of antique tapestry curtains. For a weatherboarded seaside bungalow, pick bistro style fold-up dining chairs and tables complete with peeling paint, or armchairs upholstered in faded striped canvas, to add to the seaside mood. And if you are a serious lover of vintage

OPPOSITE This 18th-century
American farmhouse, with its aged
floorboards and low ceilings, simply
had to be accessorised with old
armchairs and traditional loose
covers made from antique ticking.
A scuffed wooden table echoes the
patina of the flooring.

THIS PAGE By contrast, in this
converted Manhattan warehouse,
an eclectic mix of 20th-century
seating and a custom-made modern
table contributes to a masculine,
urban vintage mood.

pieces, you may even wish to find a home whose architectural style precisely suits an existing collection. So you may be drawn towards a 19th-century house as a fitting place for your 19th-century pressed glass, or to a Modernist home for your mid-20th-century furniture.

THRIFTY AND FUN

For nearly all of us, cost is an issue when it comes to furnishing. Students and first-time buyers should celebrate: now vintage is popular, there's no shame in using Granny's or mother's cast-off 60s dressing table or a 40s utility table and chairs, especially if you mix them with modern high-street buys. Precisely because some vintage finds are cheap, if not free, accessorising a home is less fraught: it's not the end of the world if you make a mistake — but dispose of your errors thoughtfully, taking them to your nearest charity shop.

If you like a sophisticated interior, don't cast aside vintage because you fear you'll end up with a thrift-shop look. Find your level. Invest in some beautiful

THIS PAGE Don't disregard a shabby chair just because it isn't part of a set: there is a genuine pleasure in setting it, all alone, against a wall, and enjoying its shape, its distressed finish, and wondering about its history.

OPPOSITE The more you bargain-hunt, the more you will hone your personal likes and dislikes. If you're constantly drawn to a particular genre, use it as the basis of a collection. Here, the bright colours of pennants and flags set the tone.

THIS PAGE If you're operating on a tight budget, buy just one classic 20th-century piece and show it off against plain white walls. This leather classic, the PK31/2 sofa by Poul Kjaerholm, is highly collectible.

OPPOSITE ABOVE LEFT Junk shop buys or an unusual collection can be made into a cohesive display by placing in identical frames. These mini knitwear designs add quirky humour in a home office.

OPPOSITE ABOVE RIGHT If you have a particular fondness for a certain style or subject, make it the basis of a display. In this bedroom, framed fashion illustrations add character and elegance.

classic pieces by well-known designers: many of the world's coolest homes now boast 20th-century American and European furniture and art.

And do remember to have fun. Don't worry about identifying the antiques of the future, but concentrate instead on snapping up things you love. A certain piece might appeal because it reminds you of your childhood, because it's ridiculously kitsch, or because it has a fantastical retro shape or colour that has long since disappeared off the style radar. Some of the quirkiest, most unusual finds involve pattern and print, from graphic, unusually coloured 50s textiles, through original 30s wallpaper featuring rosebuds and bluebirds, to futuristic 70s silver vinyl wallpaper. If vintage has any common themes, then irreverence, a willingness to experiment and a total lack of pretension are key.

PERSONAL
The broad new trend in interiors is to create eclectic homes – a trend that, until recently, has been rather sidelined. It's wonderful to see a return to the personal interior. Who hasn't experienced the thrill of visiting someone's home and hearing the story behind a particular table, painting or vase? The sure-fire way to create a unique home is to avoid mass-market purchases or even retro copy-cat styles, and to plunder the past for the real thing. No-one else will have the same 50s exotically veneered cocktail table or that 60s leather-and-rosewood Danish sofa. Similarly, if you arrange your flowers in an original smoked-glass 70s vase or set your party nibbles out on a 70s teak cheeseboard with a tiled inlay, you'll give your home a stamp of individuality.

Customised buys or do-it-yourself details provide an even more original touch. You can try taking your cue from one of the many design companies that bring a new twist to vintage materials, for example, by stitching silk scarves into brand new cushion covers or even converting old metal jelly moulds into pendant lampshades, complete with silk-covered flex.

ECO VINTAGE

Slowly but surely, we're all being encouraged to adopt a greener, more eco lifestyle. Buying salvaged pieces, reusing and reinventing old furniture, and passing down furniture from one generation to the next are all valid ways of doing your bit, as are swapping items with friends and selling things you don't want to vintage websites. If you try some of these approaches and always think twice before buying new, you'll have both a clearer conscience and a much more interesting home.

RE-USING OLD FURNITURE

There are manifold benefits to using old furniture. Each piece has a story to tell, from the gentle fade on a Turkish carpet to the sigh of springs on an aged sofa. Vintage pieces are often beautifully crafted in a way not seen in today's mass-produced items. Plundering past decades can also throw up quirky pieces of furniture you didn't know you needed. Think of a smoked-glass cocktail cabinet, a teak hostess trolley or a 70s coffee table that incorporates an ingenious magazine rack at one end. The important thing is to choose, or re-use, pieces that have a great sense of style.

It's also crucial to remember that vintage furniture won't be pristine: that's all part of its charm. So don't over-mend. If a piece is in a bad state of repair, it will need attention, but take care to get repairs done using traditional methods. If you're having an old sofa re-upholstered, for example, make sure that wool wadding and feather and down fillings are used, rather than cheap foam. If it's an old lampbase you're bringing back to life, traditional twisted silk flex should be used for the rewiring rather than modern plastic cable.

Vintage also means that you don't have to throw away a piece such as a single dining chair because it's no longer part of a matching set. Instead, make it the start of an interesting collection of similar chairs.

The most up-to-date way to give old furniture a fresh new twist is by clever customising. Whether that's adding a new enamelled steel top to an old pine kitchen table or upholstering a tatty Knole sofa in hot-pink denim, is up to you. There's now a new breed of inventive young upholsterers, dedicated to traditional methods but creating amazing new looks for old

ABOVE "Second-hand" is no longer a dirty word: using salvaged furniture is the ultimate eco-friendly furniture choice. Old pieces are often extremely well made, and the patina of age injects a character that new pieces do not possess.

OPPOSITE Remember, it's not always necessary to re-upholster an old sofa. Sometimes, gently faded fabric adds to the charm. Cover the odd stain or hole with patches, in a similarly distressed fabric, to give the piece a new lease of life.

sofas and armchairs. They use anything from tweed to army blankets to create a fresh twist. Some antique dealers are also following suit, often taking it upon themselves to revamp quite ordinary furniture in funky ways, from covering a Louis XV-style reproduction daybed in brightly coloured PVC to painting a curvy period console table silver.

RECYCLED TEXTILES

Until recently, few of us would have thought twice about re-using old textiles, but times have changed. Now landfill sites are groaning with cast-off fabrics that could have a perfectly good second life. Embrace the new thrift chic and consider what you have at home that you could re-use. You could, for example, cut up old-fashioned voluminous chintz festoon blinds and use them to re-cover dining-chair seats, or make new

curtains out of antique French linen sheets, perhaps trimmed with recycled fringing. Unused clothes are another source of inspiration. Old jumpers you never wear or worn denims, for example, can be fashioned into neat little scatter cushions. Second-hand curtain shops, eBay and specialist vintage textile websites make brilliant hunting grounds. And as well as textiles, look out for old trimmings, lace, buttons, beads and ribbons.

If you're not handy with a needle, don't despair: many young designers are now specialising in creating pretty home accessories using vintage or recycled textiles. You can also look out for ready-made accessories on eco websites and, increasingly, in the shops. Isn't it more satisfying to buy a cushion cover made from an old grain sack, a lavender bag or padded hanger made from offcuts of a fashion textile, or a doorstop stitched from an old pair of jeans? Washed and faded fabrics have a tactile and visual appeal that's perfect for mixing in with a shabby-chic interior and designers use patchwork, appliqué or embroidery to give them a fresh new look.

One particularly exciting textile route to follow is to seek out vintage prints. Many specialists in 20th-century antiques, from shops to websites, sell retro fabrics alongside furniture, and they often supply detailed information on the fabric designer. Rare and mint condition fabrics by named designers such as Lucienne Day now reach high prices, but it's still possible to pick up a bargain if the designer is an unknown. The muted colours, graphic patterns and charming children's prints from the 50s, 60s and 70s, look great mixed with retro and modern furniture. If you're lucky enough to find some, buy up just enough for some cushion covers or for re-upholstering a retro bar stool. For a softer look, go to a textile specialist who offers antique linens, ticking or silk off the roll.

OPPOSITE You can often only buy recycled or vintage fabrics in short, one-off lengths. These are ideal for making curtains for small windows. Here, a pretty piece of old lace with a simple heading gives privacy and filters the light.

THIS PAGE Think creatively when it comes to vintage textiles such as shawls or bed covers. In this Finnish apartment, a patchwork quilt – a family heirloom – has been turned into a dramatic curtain.

OPPOSITE A retro vintage look makes the ideal match with 20th-century architecture. But it's possible to cheat a little. In this New York apartment, classic 1929 Barcelona chairs have been teamed with a modern rug made using the colours of the 60s.

WHICH VINTAGE STYLE?

For the vintage virgin, it can be tricky to work out which retro style to choose. Although going vintage offers a certain stylistic freedom — you can mix historical periods and blend shapes and finishes — it's helpful to settle on a broad theme. Take time to review the architecture of your home, the possessions you already have, your lifestyle and the looks that attract you. Put together a mood-board, amass tear sheets from magazines, haunt innovative antique showrooms and scrutinise decorative influences in hotels or restaurants where the vintage ethic has been employed. If it turns out that mirrored furniture and waisted silk lampshades are what you like, then go for boudoir vintage; if recycled ticking bolsters and distressed painted armoires appeal, then country vintage is the one.

ABOVE A seaside home calls for appropriately distressed furniture. Here, painted tongue-and-groove panelling teams comfortably with simple, pale wood pieces. These have the lean silhouette that was a common feature of post-war furniture design.

LEFT For a raw, rustic vintage look, carry the theme of distressed finishes from wall and floor treatments, such as bare pink plaster and old slate, through to old country furniture that is gently scratched and peeling.

BELOW A country vintage interior should feel relaxed and artlessly thrown together, but pay attention to getting the look just right. The aged textiles and rustic furniture in this room look casual, but have been carefully combined.

OPPOSITE Aim for a creative combination of touchy-feely textures. In this room there is a good contrast between the roughness of the exposed brick wall and the brick fireplace, and the distressed gilded wood mirror and worn velvet upholstery.

COUNTRY VINTAGE

Relaxed, comfortable, and perfect for rustic properties, country vintage is one of the easiest looks to put together. One key component is battered old timber furniture, either with a rich patina or featuring flaky, distressed paint finishes. Match this with rough textures, from old tapestry pieces to leather-upholstered armchairs, and blend with original or recycled waxed or painted floorboards, terracotta or quarry-stone tiles, painted plaster or wood-panelled walls, and stone worktops. Add fabrics in gently muted colours, either plain or featuring a mix of stripes, checks and faded florals, and think worn velvet or striped horsehair upholstery, antique linen curtains and ticking cushion covers, and natural fibre matting or faded old kilims for the floor.

BOUDOIR VINTAGE

This look has grown in popularity just as fashion's love-affair with all thing vintage has blossomed: threadbare beauty is the theme. The mood is glamorous, so it's a particularly apt choice for bedrooms and bathrooms. Just how feminine you make it is down to personal choice. It's a look that works particularly well in a period townhouse, with high ceilings and tall windows. Here, team it with wide painted floorboards, elegant marble worktops and plenty of sparkle, including giant wall mirrors. Use subtle paint finishes or vintage floral wallpaper on one or more walls. Curvy furniture shapes suit the look, so fake gilded Louis XIV-style furniture, curvy cane chairs and generous daybeds are ideal, as are 30s mirrored dressing tables and rounded pouffes. Enhance the look with your choice of glamorous fabrics – faded silk eiderdowns, velvet cushions and lace detailing.

ABOVE Decorative details must work as hard as the principal surfaces. Here, a delicate shagreen-covered dressing table, accessorised with vintage perfume bottles and silver-mounted hairbrushes, adds essential glamour.

LEFT For a truly effective vintage boudoir look, it's crucial to introduce an element of authentic pattern, via wallpaper or fabric. Look for damask motifs, florals or stylised botanical patterns rather than graphic prints.

THIS PAGE A vintage boudoir look depends on the right mix of textures. Aim to gather together dense fabrics with a sheen, such as velvet and old satin, and combine with embroidery and lace. Delicate vintage fabrics need extra care, but do look fantastic.

You can achieve a retro vintage mood by combining furniture from one era with decorative influences from another. Here, Saarinen's classic 50s Tulip chairs are teamed with white walls and a glossy resin floor, to give a 70s space-age look.

RETRO VINTAGE

Retro vintage, with its emphasis very firmly on mid-20th-century style, is an ideal choice for anyone in search of a crisp, almost masculine look. Here the emphasis should be on the shape and style of the retro furniture and accessories, so keep the décor simple to set these off. If you want to play up a collection of stylish 30s Modernist furniture, you should team it with neutral carpet or lino on the floor and with white or pale-painted walls. For a funkier, 50s look, try combining bright pastels like sky blue or pink, with graphic original textiles and a vintage abstract rug. To get inspiration for these retro looks, finishes and surfaces, hunt out original home-style books in second-hand book dealers or on the web. They offer visual cues as well as being a great read!

ABOVE Retro vintage isn't just about 20th-century architecture. Here, the contrast of a classic 20s Barcelona chair set against 19th-century painted panelling and a neo-classical salvaged fire surround looks particularly dramatic.

RIGHT Purists will want to match furniture and accessories from a chosen period to the architecture of their home. In this 30s house, even the bedroom furniture is from the same period.

LEFT An urban vintage look is all about getting the scale right. In a converted warehouse, the furniture must be bold enough and big enough to fill the space, so look for large pieces – perhaps themselves salvaged from a factory.

OPPOSITE For a softer take on urban vintage, experiment by contrasting curvy pieces – such as this reproduction Louis XVI-style sofa – with tall ceilings. Lush textiles, like velvet or satin, also create dramatic tension between colder surfaces such as concrete.

URBAN VINTAGE

If you live in a city flat or converted warehouse, and want a grittier take on vintage, then pick an urban theme. This is the look to choose if you favour cool retro buys such as 50s American-style metal desks or lockers, second-hand neon or metal signs, or salvaged factory finds such as Victorian adjustable office shelving or giant industrial lanterns. Team these elements with robust surfaces, so think exposed brick or plain painted walls, and concrete, sheet-metal or poured-rubber floors. Urban vintage is a fun, young look that's at its most dramatic with only a few carefully chosen pieces, often on a very large scale. Choose accessories with kitsch overtones, such as an illuminated Launderette sign in the kitchen, or a framed vintage film poster, and keep fabrics to a minimum.

The defining features of today's clean-cut, modern interiors are usually plain white or polished-plaster walls, limestone or dark-wood floors, and glass or stainless-steel surfaces. If you've adopted this trend but want to add a decorative look to your boxy contemporary furniture and streamlined fitted kitchen, choosing a few vintage accessories will do the trick. Introducing the occasional quirky vintage buy, from a naïve 60s painting to a little French boudoir armchair upholstered in silk satin, will take things in a new direction. You might replace a plain drum lampshade on a simple stainless-steel base with a shade made from an original 60s print fabric, or you could use a framed 40s film poster to impart colour and pattern to a plain wall. The trick is to start gradually and play with your new vintage buys so the look evolves.

THIS PAGE It's essential to amass things you love, but try to keep a loose decorative theme in mind when you are buying. This collection looks so good because all the pieces are very representative of the popular culture of the 50s.

OPPOSITE By all means collect a mass of items of a similar nature, but keep a definite decorative purpose in mind. For example, this vast collection of simple mirrors turns ordinary, plain painted walls into a dramatic feature.

EVERY VINTAGE FIND TELLS A STORY. ASK THE SELLER IF HE OR SHE KNOWS A PIECE'S HISTORY, OR LOOK FOR AN ARTIST'S NAME OR MAKER'S MARK THAT YOU CAN RESEARCH AT YOUR LEISURE.

GOING SHOPPING

Accumulating vintage finds should be enjoyable, but it pays to keep in mind a few simple rules. Take time to research and know your sources, and build up personal contacts with your local salvage dealer, or a vintage website. A specialist is constantly trawling markets and sales, so can keep an eye out for a particular item you may be looking for. Set yourself a budget and don't get carried away. And finally, always choose something to which you're really attracted, rather than buying for investment.

FREEBIE FINDS
This is the cheapest, and often most creative way to start off a vintage collection. Poke around in or beside skips (ask permission first if it's obvious who the owner of the skip is), keep your eyes open for discarded items left on the pavement with a "take me" sign, or swap with friends. If you're not sure whether a piece is in a good state of repair, take it anyway, as you can always think about it later, and it may not be there the next day. If you find a piece that's truly beyond repair or too fragile for everyday use, perhaps you could customise it and use it decoratively, or put it to use in the garden. A giant but broken station clock, for example, would look fantastic adorning a garden wall, or you could repaint a collection of old gilded picture frames in glossy black and hung them en masse for decorative impact.

JUNK SHOPPING
Car-boot sales and junk shops offer a complete mixture of items, from cracked floral china to second-hand Welsh rugs, from wicker chairs to garish oil

paintings. Half the fun lies in picking over the stock, revelling in a dash of nostalgia, and – hopefully – finding a treasure that you love. At car-boot sales, don't be afraid to haggle over the price, request a discount if you're buying several items, or ask the seller to keep something aside while you make a final decision. It can help to take several big bags with you to carry home your booty. Look carefully for any damage and ask yourself how much that really matters. If you want a piece to be practical, then insist on good condition, but if you're buying for the look – such as a decorative tailor's dummy – then a bit of wear and tear won't matter. If you're amassing furniture or accessories from a particular period, try to choose iconic pieces that reflect the era. If you're purchasing pieces online, from a vintage website for instance, it's perfectly acceptable to ask the seller detailed questions or to request sufficient images to show off the item from all angles.

ANTIQUE SHOPPING

These days, many antique shops stock 20th-century retro furniture, accessories and fabrics, and prices are rising fast. It's easy to get swept along, so if you're buying a serious vintage piece, do ensure that it's something you really love, and take time to research prices. Find out about the particular designer or maker and whether there were any manufacturing marks that will help authenticate it as the real thing. These days, there are plenty of books dedicated to 20th-century antiques, and it can be fun to research in greater depth. And when you buy, differentiate clearly between inevitable signs of wear and tear, and actual damage. While it's fun to invest in a named designer piece, complete with its original upholstery, if you want to use the furniture every day, buying an item that's been reupholstered might make more sense.

FAKING IT

If you lack time or inclination to trawl the junk shops and salvage yards, you can always cheat. It's possible to buy modern replicas of iconic 20th-century furniture and lighting, from an Eero Saarinen Tulip dining chair to an Eileen Gray side table. But do ensure you buy high-quality versions, made to the original specifications, and not cheap copies. There are also wonderful retro kitchen appliances and accessories to be had, ranging from 50s-style American fridges and freezers to weighing scales in traditional designs. If you do buy new pieces, mix and match them with originals. That will help to create a more authentic mood.

OPPOSITE When you are buying vintage, if an item is very distressed, it can still be of decorative value. This 18th-century chair is a thing of beauty precisely because of its state of extreme wear and tear.

THIS PAGE Twentieth-century furniture can reach high prices, so if you love a particular look but can't afford the real thing, consider buying re-issues. For example, these Mies van der Rohe chairs (1929–30) were reissued by Knoll in 1960.

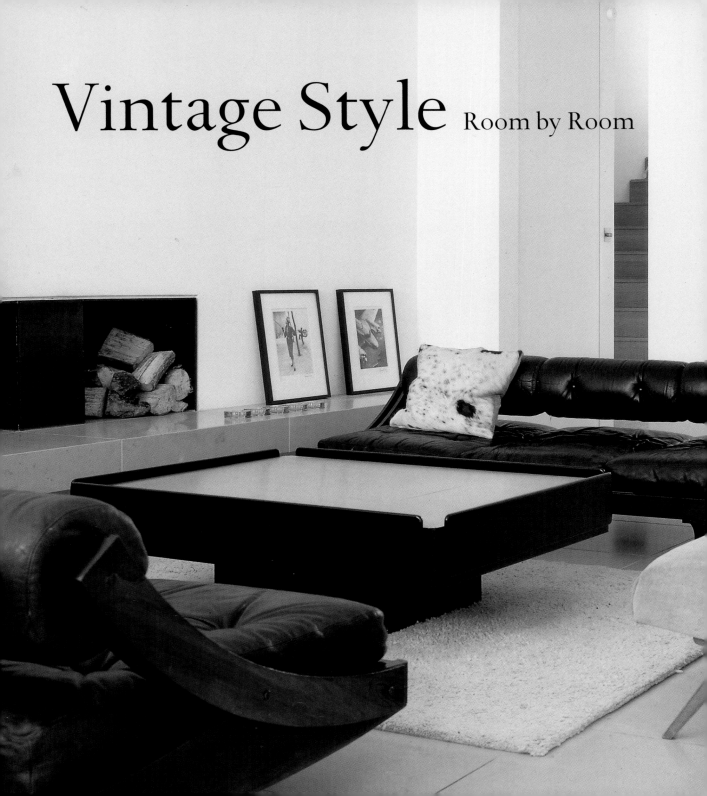

Vintage Style Room by Room

THIS PAGE It's perfectly possible to add some vintage detailing to a contemporary kitchen. In this open-plan living space, seamless modern built-in storage has been teamed with 70s sofas and a pair of 50s Italian armchairs upholstered in velvet.

Armed with a broad idea of which vintage style to choose, and where to source individual pieces, now is the time to make more detailed, practical decisions, room by room. By all means opt for Edwardian bath taps, but have them checked by a good plumber so you're sure they will work with modern plumbing. And, unless you're a complete purist and want everything in your home "as found", remember that original 50s kitchen units only make good sense if the doors open seamlessly and the surfaces are low-maintenance.

On a more aesthetic note, consider whether you will roll out the vintage look throughout, or restrict it to just one room. The easiest spaces in which to experiment are the sitting room or a bedroom, where you can start off by adding just one or two key pieces of vintage furniture. Choosing vintage as a theme throughout the home, though, will provide a sense of gentle cohesion and using old pieces will result in every room looking quite unique. As you gain in confidence, make more permanent decorative choices, whether that's using original 70s vinyl wallpaper or classic Art Deco bathroom tiles. The good news is that there are no rules to break. Choose what looks and feels right — you are not creating a museum — and bear in mind that, in high-traffic areas such as halls and kitchens, brand new, robust floor and wall finishes will provide the most hardwearing background to your vintage treasures.

OPPOSITE ABOVE LEFT For a formal sitting room, bring vintage Victorian armchairs up to date with a chic, dark colour scheme and tailored upholstery.

OPPOSITE ABOVE RIGHT In this elegant bathroom, an early 20th-century copper bath takes centre stage and contrasts well with the grey marble surround.

OPPOSITE CENTRE LEFT Here, the rich patina of a reclaimed wooden worktop works well with crisp new stainless-steel bowls.

OPPOSITE CENTRE RIGHT Vintage tableware is easy and inexpensive to collect. Here, it's perfect for an everyday table setting.

OPPOSITE BELOW LEFT If you are in search of a romantic hideaway bedroom, look for a pretty antique headboard to team with a selection of vintage linens and bedcovers.

OPPOSITE BELOW RIGHT Vintage style is as much about mixing, as it is about matching. Here, a Knoll table bought in Paris has been accessorised with leather dining chairs in a very different style.

KITCHENS AND EATING ZONES

BELOW For a quirky feel, keep built-in units simple and let the emphasis fall - as it does here - on industrial-style chairs and a table that takes centre-stage. A mix of textures, from stainless steel to salvaged timber floorboards, enhances the mood.

Most people have a firm idea of the type of kitchen they want. For some, modernity and a clutter-free environment are crucial: the kitchen is a work-zone above all else, with food and gadgets concealed from view. Others love a homely, cosy kitchen, filled with favourite things, from books to furniture and from crockery to cooking utensils. Open shelves and dressers find favour with such people. For a few, having an authentic old kitchen is the ultimate goal, be that the original kitchen units from a 60s flat, say, or a mix-and-match creation combining, for instance, an old butcher's block, a Victorian pine dresser and an oak refectory table for a country vintage look. Now is the time to decide: which type of kitchen person are you?

The good news for split-personality vintage fans who want a streamlined contemporary kitchen (but who still love kitsch period buys) is that these days it has become commonplace to combine an open-plan kitchen with a breakfast bar, or if there's space, with a dining area. Choosing vintage style

OPPOSITE To create a vintage flavour without authentic units, have kitchen doors made to order in a funky finish. In this Manhattan loft, optical laminate has been used for the cupboard fronts. Together with brightly coloured chairs and quirky accessories, this loosely creates a 70s space-age theme.

gives you the chance for something that works across both the kitchen and the dining areas. With clever planning, you can easily mix a modern kitchen, for example, with a rustic 19th-century cherrywood dining table and original 60s polypropylene chairs: the fun lies in the contrast. Or, if you are 100 per cent committed to salvage buys, the deliberate mix of multi-purpose pieces of furniture in both areas – for example, antique pine tables with industrial steel trolleys, and perhaps a painted French dresser – effectively blurs the boundaries between the cooking and eating zones.

KITCHEN UNITS

For the style purist, the only type of kitchen to have is an original old one. Fitted kitchens came into favour from the 20s onwards, and were particularly popular from the 50s. Some salvage yards specialise in sourcing the popular 50s English Rose and Boulton and Paul kitchens, and will strip and re-spray them for you. For an authentic 50s look, go for bright primary colours, though natural wood finishes were also popular at the time. It's also worth scouring the internet for vintage kitchens, though you will often be buying "as seen".

Disadvantages of buying an original kitchen are that old drawer runners and stained worktops will need replacing and that modern appliances are too deep for the units. As an alternative, consider teaming your units with a freestanding retro-style fridge and dishwasher, or find a kitchen supplier who can offer a replica of a 50s-style fitted kitchen.

A more relaxed, country vintage style calls for a mix-and-match approach. Scour reclamation yards, junk stores and car boot sales for cupboards, shelves, dressers and tables that you can combine to create the look, but plan carefully to avoid a chaotic effect. For instance, by choosing cupboards and shelves in the same material or by using the same worktop throughout, it will help to blend a mixture of distressed furniture. If you employ a creative carpenter to install everything, he will ensure that pieces can be tailored to suit the space.

When it comes to choosing a sink, opt for one that is in keeping: look for inexpensive reclaimed ceramic Butler's sinks, or even older stone sinks. Once these are sandblasted, they are robust and good-looking.

Of course, we don't all have the chance (or the inclination) to install a vintage kitchen. If you want a brand new kitchen, but in a retro style, some kitchen companies now offer good authentic copies, or get a

OPPOSITE For a casual kitchen/dining room aim for an "evolved" look. Here, a variety of different elements – the chunky industrial-style lighting, rack shelving, big clock and unfitted electrical appliances – sit very comfortably together.

BELOW Mixing modern and vintage can work very well in a kitchen. Here, the plain white units and pale floor act as a foil for the well-worn surfaces of the old school-style chairs and the modest zinc-topped kitchen table.

joiner to create one to your design. For a seaside vintage look, consider cabinet doors made with tongue-and-groove panels, while a rustic country kitchen looks good with painted doors or with a stained-wood finish. Minor adjustments to an existing kitchen are also possible. If you have plain, wooden units, you can still create a shabby-chic effect by replacing new knobs with antique iron handles, by swapping a modern laminate worktop with a reclaimed iroko hardwood surface, or by choosing freestanding retro electrical appliances instead of contemporary integrated versions.

LEFT Try accessorising a worn table-top with old linen, china and glass.

OPPOSITE ABOVE LEFT Matching Alvar Aalto furniture looks formal.

OPPOSITE ABOVE RIGHT A 30s table and 60s chairs are unified by the red in the Donald Judd print.

OPPOSITE BELOW LEFT Classic chairs and a table stand out against white.

OPPOSITE BELOW RIGHT Here, classic Scandinavian modern steel-framed chairs are casually mixed with 19th-century chairs.

DINING FURNITURE

If there's room in the kitchen for a dining table, then you have two choices – a contrast with the kitchen units or both in a similar style vein. Next consider what shape table you would like and whether the table must double for food preparation or is just for dining, which means that a more delicate tabletop is acceptable. Next consider your choice of vintage style. A scratched enamelled worktop is perfect for a shabby-chic look, while for a groovy mid-20th-century vibe, consider an original 20th-century design, such as an Eero Saarinen pedestal table. In a small city flat, an original 50s dinette set, complete with Formica top and chairs in tubular steel and vinyl, would fit the bill perfectly.

Don't just select seating on the basis of looks: comfort and practicality are also important, so if your vintage buys have wobbly legs or ripped upholstery, then have them repaired. You may be lucky enough to find a matching set of chairs, but this will put up the price. Less expensive options are to choose stacking-style or utility chairs, to pick a generic type – such as old French café metal chairs or classic Windsor chairs – or, to unify a mismatched set of wooden chairs, paint them all one colour or re-upholster in matching – preferably vintage – fabric.

Bench seating is more flexible and more informal. For a country-style home, experiment with lightly distressed garden benches piled high with cushions, or for an industrial-style apartment, look in a salvage yard for items such as leather-upholstered hospital seating or old church pews. Stools are fun and can be useful. You can pick up well-priced post-war utility breakfast stools upholstered in their original graphic-print oilcloth, or, if you have more money to spend, go for European Modernist leather-and-chrome bar stools or vintage Swedish high-back swivel chairs.

SIDEBOARDS AND DRESSERS

The mid-20th-century fashion for sideboards has returned with a vengeance, and with good reason. A sideboard is extremely practical: as well as being able to hold tableware and cutlery, it's also a great place for hiding a stereo, as well as providing a useful surface for decorative accessories. Particularly good buys are slim 50s, 60s and 70s sideboards from Scandinavia, in characteristic woods such as rosewood and teak.

The traditional dresser, most commonly cluttered with cups, plates and jugs, has a place in the country vintage kitchen, and offers a more decorative alternative than plain shelves or cupboards. Many antique shops and reclamation yards have them in

finishes ranging from distressed paint to waxed pine, and they needn't cost a fortune. The classic country dresser is loaded with a haphazard mix of glass and china in a variety of patterns and colours, but for a more modern look, stick to plain china, all in one colour, and / or vintage glass. A dresser can also provide you with a great place to display your kitchenware collection – anything from old willow-pattern china to cabbageware. A massed display of your treasures will make a strong statement.

FLOORS AND WALLS

Whatever vintage kitchen style you're aiming for, pick appropriate flooring that will be hard-wearing. Dip into style books of a particular era to get ideas: linoleum, cork tiles or rubber are perfect for a mid-20th-century look, while for a scrubbed country vintage mood, the best choices are salvaged timber floorboards, reclaimed terracotta tiles, or flagstones. New materials can work well, too. Modern slate has a nicely riven finish that is perfect with a distressed country pine kitchen, while a new concrete floor makes a great backdrop for old factory furniture in an urban vintage kitchen.

If your taste for vintage verges on the kitsch, then look at the vinyl wallpapers of the 50s and 60s, many of which were decorated with graphic fruits and vegetables. If you can find some original paper of the era, it will look perfect on a single wall – perhaps the one nearest to the dining table – contrasted with plain painted walls elsewhere in the room.

Brand new glossy wall tiles will feel at odds with vintage cupboards and dining accessories. Instead, try tongue-and-groove panelling: painted white or blue-grey to suit a seaside vintage mood, or stained in a dark tone, it makes a great contrast to bright, groovy 60s retro furniture. Since salvaged tiles are not often

OPPOSITE A freestanding sideboard or dresser adds infinitely more character to a kitchen/dining room than a run of faceless built-in storage cupboards. Look for old shop cabinets if you want an industrial-style alternative.

THIS PAGE It's worth the effort of sourcing a salvaged floor for a kitchen, whether it's recycled floorboards with a great patina, terracotta tiles or old flagstones. Distressed surfaces look particularly appropriate with old, scuffed furniture and recycled worktops.

available in large quantities, you may come up with some creative solutions by combining old with new and playing with contrasts. In similar vein, a few 18th-century Delft tiles, even if they are slightly chipped, will look fantastic as a modest splashback over a stone sink.

ELECTRICAL APPLIANCES

Sleek built-in kitchen appliances have become so ubiquitous that it's easy to forget that kitchen appliances were once freestanding and bulky. Modern retro-styled appliances are now very popular and with good reason. These are better buys than old appliances as you will be able to choose environmentally friendly versions with the best energy ratings. Though some mid-20th-century US manufacturers tried to emulate the colours and styles of cars of that time, most electrical appliances were typically white or cream.

OPPOSITE For a 50s mood, team unfitted electrical appliances with colourful worktops, or opt for new retro-styled American fridges or dishwashers in funky colours and with pleasing rounded contours.

RIGHT A range-style cooker instantly creates a period look. New versions are the most eco-friendly: pick stainless steel for an industrial vintage look or find a specialist who will create a custom- colour enamel to match your kitchen.

Nowadays, though, you can buy retro American-style fridges and dishwashers in sweetie colours, as well as stainless-steel range-style cookers. If you are a purist, you can, of course find reconditioned appliances, but always buy from a specialist supplier. Such appliances were built to last, so they were often simply designed and easy to maintain. If you find an old appliance, you can have it re-sprayed in a colour of your choice at the same time as it is being reconditioned.

While scouring vintage websites, you'll also find smaller electrical appliances on offer, such as 60s blenders or toasters. It can be fun to seek these out, especially if they are in good condition and perhaps in their original box, but do ensure that you have them checked before use by a reputable electrician. If you can bear not to use them, it's probably safer just to have them on show and enjoy them as collector's items.

TABLEWARE AND ACCESSORIES

The appeal of the identikit table setting has waned and now it's much more fun to set your table with an inventive selection of vintage glass, tableware and cutlery. It not only looks fantastic but will also be a talking point. What's more, it's also comparatively inexpensive and easy to source, particularly at car boot sales and junk shops. Antique cutlery, for example, has a pleasing weight, comes in classic designs, and can often be bought by the bundle quite reasonably. In addition to everyday tableware, look out for unusual table accessories that will make a bold statement – from celery vases to silver hot-water jugs, and from silver salt cellars to lazy Susans. Match your choices to your vintage style or mix styles together. For a vintage urban dinner setting, team 50s single-colour ceramics with graphic 60s designs. For a relaxed country theme, combine antique willow-pattern plates with red Victorian water glasses. For fun at teatime, mix hand-painted 30s teacups and saucers with pastry knives featuring pastel-coloured handles.

Tablelinens are also easy to collect. Fine linens can be expensive, so instead scour junk stores and country-house sales for classic choices such as antique linen sheets, perhaps monogrammed, that you can cut down and use as tablecloths or napkins. For a more casual retro vintage look, hunt out quirky 50s oilcloth – great for a kitchen table – look for 70s napkins printed with the big flowers of the era, or, for the ultimate kitsch look, snap up a hand-knitted tea cosy.

LEFT Many mid-20th-century vintage tables were made in sculptural shapes, so try not to cover them up with a tablecloth. Instead, look out for mats and napkins of the era, designed to enhance a bare tabletop.

OPPOSITE If you have stuck very closely to period styling from a particular era – this American home is furnished entirely with pieces made between 1920 and 1940 – then it makes sense to have tableware of the same era, too.

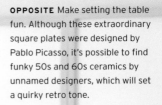

OPPOSITE Make setting the table fun. Although these extraordinary square plates were designed by Pablo Picasso, it's possible to find funky 50s and 60s ceramics by unnamed designers, which will set a quirky retro tone.

THIS PAGE During the mid-20th-century, there was a particular vogue for glassware in very simple shapes and in smoky colours, including grey and toffee shades. It looks surprisingly contemporary even today, so works well when mixed with modern plates.

GENTLE COLOURS AND
SOFTLY FADED VINTAGE
FURNISHINGS ADD A
NOSTALGIC CHARM TO THE
LIVING ROOM. MAKE THIS
A SPACE FOR RELAXATION:
ENJOY DRESSING IT UP WITH
FLOWERS AND TREASURES.

ABOVE In this dramatic, highly decorative boudoir vintage drawing room, the glamour derives not just from the mix of curvy, elaborately upholstered furniture, but also from the confident use of damask vintage wallpaper. Plain painted floorboards lighten the look.

OPPOSITE An eclectic mix of furniture can work if you keep your nerve and go for bold elements. Here, turquoise fringing on a red velvet sofa, a zebra skin on the floor, and floral wallpaper teamed with plain walls, are perfectly in balance.

LIVING ROOMS

While it's rare these days to have a formal drawing room, many of us still want a relaxed sitting room separate from the kitchen/dining space. Choosing vintage style here can only enhance the ambience: after all, who wouldn't feel at peace surrounded by soft, gently worn textiles and well-loved furniture? The living room is also the perfect spot for vintage virgins to experiment, because it is the key part of the home for displaying personal treasures or favourite pieces of inherited furniture.

Instead of cluttering up your living room up, concentrate on editing everything that goes in. Start by deciding how formal a look you want, based on who uses the room, and for what, then consider your style. In a boudoir-style living room, little gilt chairs, velvet upholstery and chandeliers are perfect. A relaxed, country vintage mood can be created with a mix of distressed leather armchairs, a faded Aubusson rug and floral cushions, while

for a retro vintage look, mix mid- to late-20th-century furniture - with spindly legs and unusual wood grains - with graphic 50s fabrics and funky lighting. A vintage industrial look will rely heavily on one or two pieces of unusual salvaged furniture, perhaps upholstered in modern printed cotton, together with raw surfaces such as plastered walls and plain wooden floorboards.

WALLS

In the vintage home, choosing a wall finish isn't just about adding pattern or colour. Walls need to enhance well-loved furniture and accessories, not conflict with them. Your choice is either to create a deliberate contrast or go for a cohesive look. For example, walls

ABOVE A distressed paint finish is a way of unifying walls and gently aged furniture. In this London drawing room, the wall panelling has a dark craquelure finish, which forms a strongly dramatic background for a feathered head-dress and a bold 40s armchair.

LEFT In a sophisticated drawing room, with the emphasis on gently faded velvet or silk, choose a textural wall covering that still looks smart. Smooth polished plaster is an ideal choice, especially teamed with a sparkling Venetian mirror.

OPPOSITE A textural wall covering adds softness to a mix of distressed furnishings and furniture. In a funky room with 70s furniture, hessian walls would be particularly authentic, or for a more elegant look, as in this sitting room, choose a smart grass cloth.

painted in a dramatic colour such a bright orange or turquoise will highlight the distressed finish of worn-in pieces like old gilded furniture or a scratched enamel light fitting. On the other hand, a muted or sombre palette of putty pinks, shades of biscuit and off-white goes nicely with a shabby chic look. If you are decoratively brave, you can even leave old plaster walls or peeling faded wallpaper "as found".

Unless you want a stark contrast, avoid bright white walls and if you're not sure how to pick a paint colour, use a manufacturer's chart. Many group colours into specific periods, from Victorian (dark reds, greens and rich ochres) to Art Deco (pale blues, greens, grey and pink). For a 50s look, experiment with red, black, yellow or lime, or the softer option of pale blues and pistachio green. Typical 60s colours included red and purple, while in the 70s, orange and brown reigned supreme.

ABOVE LEFT Painted walls are excellent for showing off unusual retro textures, such as a fitted shag-pile carpet and glittery fire surround. In this American home, plain walls also highlight the curves of a flea-market chaise longue.

ABOVE Your choices for walls may even be inspired by a key piece of retro furniture. Here, in a small flat in Paris, glass partitions are combined with painted walls: the straight lines perfectly match the cubic outline of this classic Le Corbusier leather chair.

OPPOSITE LEFT Carefully consider the balance of texture when choosing walls and flooring to team with vintage furniture. In a more sophisticated sitting room, such as this, a fine-textured sisal is a better choice than rough coir.

OPPOSITE RIGHT If you are mixing ultra-modern floor-to-ceiling glass with retro furniture, it's a good idea to use a rug in a vintage design to tie everything together. For a quick cheat, look for a modern rug that has a period design.

Consider the texture of the paint as well as its colour; a soft, matt finish looks prettiest with worn-out fabrics, while shiny gloss paint looks cool with funky 60s or 70s furniture and vintage textiles.

Patterned wallpaper is a shortcut to creating a period feel in the living room. Many specialist dealers, mainly internet-based, stock original 20th-century wallpapers. Those from the the 30s often featured tiny floral prints or larger flower designs, while in the 50s to the 70s, boldly coloured graphic prints were in vogue. Use vintage wallpaper with a light touch, restricting it to just one wall or an alcove. If, during your home renovations, you happen to discover some old wallpaper on a wall, you can have as many rolls of it as you like digitally recreated by a specialist company.

If you want a shabby-chic antique look, there are plenty of new wallpapers based on authentic 18th- or 19th-century designs, hand-blocked for a gently aged effect. But for a retro vintage sitting room, with a late 20th-century theme, you can also find modern interpretations of psychedelic, brightly coloured 60s Pop Art designs, space-age silver wallpapers, or that much-loved classic from the 70s, paper-backed hessian.

The days of complex paint finishes are long gone, but a textured or distressed look for walls, even on just one feature wall, is unusual and suits vintage style. Polished plaster is expensive but, teamed with faded silk curtains, is fantastic in a boudoir-style sitting room, while in a converted industrial space, consider using stone cladding or retaining the exposed brick walls. Either is perfect as a foil to cracked leather upholstery and reclaimed timber flooring. Modern wallpapers also offer the opportunity to cheat a little: think faux concrete, stone or wood panelling.

FLOORING

Getting the texture, shade and pattern of flooring right matters as much as the walls. In an older property, if you have original floorboards, so much the better. For a rustic or seaside mood, simple is good, so just sand and wax the boards, while for a more masculine or industrial-style home, use a dark wood stain or grey or black paint. If the boards are beyond repair, reclamation yards and antique timber flooring specialists are the best sources for second-hand floorboards. While you're buying, ask about the origin of the boards; it's always more fun if you know the story behind vintage items. Parquet flooring, popular in the 20s and 30s, makes a change from traditional floorboards and is an authentic choice with Art Deco furniture. And though most of us

wouldn't choose stone for a living-room floor, if you have worn flagstones or terracotta tiles in a country property, lay a rug on top and enjoy their aged patina.

For a modern living room, with 20th-century furniture, there are other hard flooring possibilities. After the war, as well as wood flooring and linoleum, cork tiles were widely used, in natural shades or colours. You can still buy both cork and linoleum today. They feel warm underfoot and they're eco-friendly and natural, too.

Natural-fibre flooring, carpet or rugs are the obvious choices if you prefer a softer feel underfoot. Sisal, coir and jute all have an uneven weave and slightly rough texture, so they go well with worn surfaces and grainy textures, though the fibres feel

LEFT In a room with organic shaped mid 20th-century furniture, which deserves to be shown off, choose hard flooring. In this airy drawing room, Saarinen Womb chairs and stools, and a Tulip table, are cleverly placed to make the most of their attractive silhouettes.

OPPOSITE Sleek fitted carpet is an excellent choice to mix with funky 20th-century furniture. Here, bright yellow upholstery and red shag-pile cushions breathe new life into classic Mies van der Rohe chairs, while the dark carpet acts as an excellent foil.

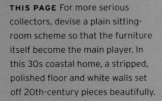

THIS PAGE For more serious collectors, devise a plain sitting-room scheme so that the furniture itself become the main player. In this 30s coastal home, a stripped, polished floor and white walls set off 20th-century pieces beautifully.

softer when mixed with wool. Traditional rush floor matting - sometimes known as medieval matting - has a particularly rough weave and a sweet smell. It looks amazing with distressed furnishings, and is great for a country or seaside vintage look. Natural-fibre flooring can be fitted to create a good, neutral background for distressed furniture or it can be made into a rug with a contrast border of, for example, suede or leather, cotton or linen. Wall-to-wall carpet is the perfect choice for a 50s vintage mood, while if you're feeling brave, a shag-pile fitted carpet is what you need for a 70s theme.

If you want a look that predates the 50s, your best choice is hard flooring and rugs. Though many old rugs are costly, if you're prepared to put up with faded or threadbare areas, it's still possible to find well-priced examples, though check for signs of moths before you buy. For a country vintage setting, keep your eye open for Aubusson carpets with traditional floral designs, Middle-Eastern woven kilims, and needlepoint rugs. If you're opting for a retro vintage look with mid-20th-century furniture, then choose a rug to match. Art Deco rugs featured large geometric patterns, often with borders and there was also a fashion for animal-skin rugs. In the 50s, rugs with graphic patterns were again popular, but in muted colours, while in the 60s and 70s, rugs were a riot of colour and abstract shapes.

FURNITURE

The appeal of vintage furniture is that there are no rules and you don't have to adhere to a set period. In fact, if you mix a few modern pieces with older ones, you'll have a look that appears to have evolved over time. Balancing modern and vintage also creates some great contrasts, for example, between a 50s leather chaise longue and a Victorian tea table, or between a twinkly 20s glass chandelier and a chunky 70s corner sofa.

Try to stick to key shapes or certain finishes so you don't end up with a haphazard jumble. In a retro vintage sitting room, for example, the characteristic long lean shapes and spindly legs of the second half of the 20th century will help to hold everything together. Similarly, a collection of delicate mismatched vintage reproduction Louis-style salon chairs, with carved wood frames and upholstered seats and backs, will all work well together. Using just one or two key upholstery fabrics is another way of adding cohesion, as is choosing similar furniture finishes. For example, in an industrial-style open-plan living room, shiny patinated metal furniture, coloured enamel finishes and bright plastics together create a cohesive look.

Remember, too that there's a fine line between worn and useless, so before you buy, check for damage and torn upholstery, as well as for practicality. An old armchair may be cosy and enveloping, but is that because its springs have gone? A narrow vintage sofa

ABOVE A living room must work practically, as well as looking good, so storage is key. It's still possible to pick up freestanding teak or rosewood bookcases, popular in the 50s and 60s, for a reasonable price.

RIGHT If you love the style of a certain vintage period, but can't match it with original period furniture, interpret the look loosely instead. These Far-Eastern chairs and table hark back to the generous curves of the Art Deco era.

OPPOSITE A vintage suite can look old-fashioned, but not when it's been given a fresh spin. The brightly coloured upholstery in this room turns a classic, subdued drawing room into a much more inventive space.

may look great, but is it sufficiently comfortable to lounge on? Is that table with the elegant tapered legs sturdy enough to withstand daily use?

You should also ensure that people can still move around your living room. Some older furniture is simply too cumbersome for today's accommodation: consider the massive proportions of a Victorian mahogany bookcase, or a generously stuffed 20s sofa. And you also might like to leave some space so that when that 30s burr-walnut cocktail cabinet appears in a junk shop or a wonderful 60s rosewood sideboard catches your eye, there's still somewhere to fit it in.

Providing adequate storage is also vital. Early on, consider whether to invest in discreet built-in storage, which leaves the emphasis on your vintage furniture and possessions, or whether to use mix-and-match retro or reclaimed storage pieces as part of an eclectic look. In a period cottage with fireplace alcoves, for example, you can enjoy the convenience of built-in cupboards, but have the doors made from recycled timber panelling. A boudoir vintage sitting room in a Victorian townhouse with tall ceilings can also benefit from seamless built-in storage, concealed behind mirrored doors or MDF doors with period mouldings.

Mid-20th-century architecture looks good with freestanding neat spindly-legged sideboards and tall narrow bookshelves from the same era. The vogue in the 50s for open-plan rooms produced clever examples of modular freestanding storage, with cupboards and shelves that are accessible from both sides, while by the 60s and 70s, built-in storage had become popular again. For an industrial vintage look, where the mood is intentionally dramatic and quirky, you can afford to make unusual choices, from a converted glass-fronted dentist's cabinet - perfect for displaying treasures - to a bookshelf constructed from Victorian office shelving.

THIS PAGE If furniture is from disparate periods and in varying styles, it's essential to create a unified look. In this peaceful drawing room, glazed grey walls and neutral upholstery do the trick.

Vintage wallpapers

- ■ To create an authentic period colour scheme, use a piece of vintage wallpaper as a starting point, then weave two or three key shades from the design into your room.

- ■ You can use retro wallpaper in a kitchen or bathroom, but opt for 50s or 60s vinyl papers with a moisture-resistant plastic coating.

- ■ Three to five rolls will paper a feature wall. Vintage papers come in the same size as today's papers – rolls of 10m x 0.53m (33ft x 21in).

Vintage wallpaper provides an opportunity to inject authentic retro style into a room. Specialist websites offer original patterns, from Victorian florals to 70s graphic designs, but most suppliers will only have a few rolls available in any one design. Consider using these limited quantities to paper a feature wall or twin fireplace alcoves, or use in a small room like a home office or nursery (you can find some charming, nostalgic vintage children's wallpapers). Older wallpapers were usually created by layering on one ink at a time, which creates a hand-painted look. Their colours shouldn't fade, but try to keep them out of direct sunlight. Later 20th-century wallpapers may be pre-pasted, but it's a safer bet to hang them using an extra-strong paste.

THIS PAGE, ABOVE AND RIGHT Not all 60s and 70s wallpapers were brightly coloured: stripes, graphics and abstracts came in muted greys and browns, too.

OPPOSITE There's a vast choice of floral vintage wallpapers, but it's the scale, colours and style of flowers that sets the tone for a given period. Here, large stylised blooms suggest a 70s mood.

BEDROOMS

The bedroom is such a personal space that it's vital to think what you want from it long before you choose a style. Some people just want a place to sleep, so barely need more than a bed and a wardrobe. Others want a subdued chill-out zone, while others like an environment full of all their favourite things. Vintage style suits all these possibilities.

THE BED

Whether you've inherited an old bed or are buying vintage, the bed must not only satisfy your eye and be in the vintage style you want, but it must be practical. Take a tape measure when you're shoppping as old beds are mostly 135cm (4ft 6in) wide or narrower (compared with today's usual 150cm/5ft) and many are a standard 190cm (6ft 3in) in length, though some older ones are shorter. If you like a long bed, you may have to have it lengthened. Most specialist antique bed dealers have a wide range in stock and many have their own workshops and can adapt your chosen bed to the right size, and provide a custom-made mattress if required. They can also add a new base and can

OPPOSITE For a dream boudoir bedroom, it's important to mix sparkly surfaces with florals and a dramatic antique bed. This one, with its Louis XV-style upholstered headboard, is perfect. A vintage 30s wallpaper, with silver-foil backing, delivers extra opulence.

BELOW LEFT In this 70s house in France, a circular bed is paired with 60s chairs in orange Plexiglass for a dramatic look, which proves that a bedroom can deliver the same design punch as a sitting room.

BELOW Urban vintage works in a bedroom, but give it an elegant twist. Here, glossy floors and a glamorously fringed bedcover contrast with bare brick walls and industrial lighting .

strip, repaint or polish the bed to your specification. Most can also also reupholster a headboard. A prettily faded one will contribute to the vintage look, but if it's torn or stained, reupholster it using a vintage fabric or, for a great contrast, a bright modern fabric.

If you're buying from a country-house sale or junk shop, look out for ugly restoration work – some beds have been cut in half and "stretched" – and inspect the base to see if it needs replacing. Wooden beds often simply need a good polish or to be repainted, but if you're considering a damaged bergère headboard, remember that repairs to canework can be expensive.

YOUR BEDROOM IS A HAVEN, SO FOCUS ATTENTION ON GENTLE COLOURS, SOFT, WORN TEXTURES, COCOONING PIECES AND PLEASING SILHOUETTES.

OPPOSITE FAR LEFT
Though very simple in style, this antique four-poster bed sets the tone perfectly in a country interior. A canopied bed can appear fussy and old-fashioned, but plain, soft vintage linen curtains look fresh and young.

OPPOSITE LEFT Gently ruched silk curtains make a glamorous bedroom, but if you cannot find sufficient vintage fabric, then use new silk and add a vintage look using scatter cushions covered with old textiles.

RIGHT For a pared-down, relaxed vintage look in a small bedroom, it can be overpowering to use a dramatic headboard. In this room, a display of 20th-century artwork on a shelf behind the bed provides a modest focal point.

A double bed takes centre stage, so take time to choose the right style. An old bed with a padded headboard is great if you like to work on your laptop in bed, but comfort-lovers may prefer a romantic four-poster. Vintage French beds — from curvy rococo to the classic lit bateau and bergère styles — are particularly decorative, especially for a boudoir look. The frame may be gilded, painted or polished. For a classic English country look, consider a brass or iron bedstead or an Edwardian bed, with a simple wood-slatted headboard. It's harder to find original 50s, 60s and 70s beds, but trawl the internet and you might be lucky. If you're an industrial vintage fan, consider a hospital-style bed — single size only — or use a salvaged door or a large antique mirror as a headboard for a plain divan.

DRESSING THE BED
It's very romantic to sleep between soft, antique linen sheets or beneath a 30s satin eiderdown. Most truly antique bedlinens need tender loving care, but old linen sheets just get better the more they're washed and can even go in the washing machine. And though linen sheets are the ultimate, cotton sheets, especially if they're prettily monogrammed, also look delightful.

Different second-hand buys suits different looks. For a country or seaside vintage bedroom, layer embroidered cotton pillowcases or those made from faded ticking. A plainer, but grander boudoir look can be achieved with outsize drawn-threadwork pillowcases, while for a funky late-20th-century mood, raid vintage websites and car boot sales for big floral-patterned polycotton sheet, duvet and pillowcase sets. Old Welsh blankets and patchwork quilts suit a rustic vintage look, and if you're handy with a needle, making your own patchwork quilt is a great way to use up scraps of vintage fabric.

THE DRESSING TABLE

The dressing table is back in vogue, which is good news if you want a dash of bedroom frivolity. For an elegant bedroom, choose a mirrored Art Deco dressing table (or a copy of one) with a velvet-upholstered pouffe. In a modern bedroom, opt for a 60s mahogany G-plan dressing table with a triple mirror, or for a bohemian look, consider a Victorian or Edwardian marble-topped washstand teamed with an old gilded mirror.

A less-than-perfect old dressing table can easily be made good with a new glass top, a lick of paint – unless it's a collector's item – or a fresh "skirt" if you happen to have a kitsch kidney-shaped table.

STORAGE

Furniture isn't just about good looks and trends: it also reflects the lifestyle of its particular era, so when you choose to go vintage, you may need to compromise. For instance, many of us are now so accustomed to built-in wardrobes that the thought of squeezing all our clothes, shoes and accessories into a freestanding wardrobe seems daunting. Make a choice. Either have built-in wardrobes and team them with one or two

If you're going to use original very old pieces, then be prepared for some basic running repairs, from darning small holes to replacing torn lace. Remember too, that older linens won't necessarily all come in standard sizes, and that duvet covers are a fairly recent invention. Often the most sensible compromise is to mix and match, using plain white modern sheets, then dressing the bed with more delicate items.

This approach is perfect if you're going vintage as you can build up a collection of covers, bedspreads and quilts. Satin, paisley or floral cotton eiderdowns and antique silk shawls give an appealing period look, and there are specialist companies who can refill old eiderdowns with new feather and down, or create a brand new one in a period design.

OPPOSITE A dressing table and mirror are essential in a boudoir-style bedroom. Provided the mirror looks glamorous (it's often possible to pick up a gilded second-hand mirror at a bargain price), the table itself can be very simple.

THIS PAGE For the Modernists of the earlier 20th century, simplicity of line was all. To achieve a similar look, get a carpenter to build a slim, wall-mounted "table" like this one. This dressing room was originally designed in the 30s.

really beautiful pieces, such as a 19th-century mahogany linen press, or site a walk-in wardrobe in another room, such as the bathroom or on a landing. Or you can give a shabby-chic look to your built-in wardrobes by using reclaimed timber for the doors or by adding vintage mirror panels.

For the purist, the only solution is to buy and use old furniture. Do look inside when buying to see if minor repairs are needed, and bear in mind the possibility of making modifications, for example, taking out shelves to provide more hanging space.

If you're keen on a particular period, it is possible to pick up a matching bedroom suite, but though it's rare to find a pair of identical wardrobes, two in a similar style, painted the same colour, will look smartly symmetrical. But a mix of periods and finishes can be more interesting. For a relaxed country look invest in a distressed painted French armoire or a plain antique

pine cupboard, or for a boudoir mood, choose a decoratively carved armoire. A run of slim metal school lockers looks very cool in an industrial setting.

SOMEWHERE TO SIT

Even in the smallest of bedrooms there's an advantage to having a quiet sitting area, whether it's a side chair or a small sofa. Make the most of the unique, one-offs you might find in junk shops or on vintage websites. A good-looking leather and mahogany dining chair is perfect in a man's dressing room, and you can often find a low Victorian or Edwardian nursing chair that would fit neatly into a small bedroom. For a shabby-chic look, try a Gustavian daybed, upholstered in antique ticking, or for the ultimate boudoir bedroom, choose a faded velvet chaise longue. If you have the space, place an attractive sofa or chair in a bay window or against a wall to show off its contours, or if your

THIS PAGE If you want glamour, ensure that every element has a dash of elegance. Here, the coloured glass chandelier, the mirrored chest of drawers and the fine curve of the armchair and stool make for a beautifully feminine 30s-style room.

OPPOSITE BELOW LEFT
Pick a comfortable bedroom armchair that will contribute decoratively to the mood of the room. In this small white-on-white bedroom, a groovy chair with circular contours echoes the contours of the 70s stacking storage system designed by Anna Castelli.

OPPOSITE BELOW RIGHT
There is precious little space in this bedroom, but by keeping to a pale colour scheme and a combination of woods with a similar tone, it still feels tranquil. A shag-pile rug adds a retro vintage mood.

THIS PAGE For a teenage girl's bedroom, put together a funkier version of a vintage boudoir style. With its period framed fashion illustrations, double bed and sugared-almond colour scheme, this bedroom exudes youthful elegance.

OPPOSITE RIGHT Not all children want to live in a sea of bright colours and clutter. For an older boy or girl, take inspiration from the spare lines and muted colours that were typically used in a 30s interior.

OPPOSITE FAR RIGHT The exuberant patterns common to the 60s and 70s make a great starting point for a younger child's room. This bedroom is dominated by a classic Marimekko print blind and a fun, 70s shag-pile rug.

bedroom is blessed with a window seat, fill it with cushions in a pleasing mix of old, faded fabrics.

CHILDREN'S ROOMS

Choosing a vintage theme for a child's room has its advantages. You can indulge in a spot of nostalgia by using furniture, wallpaper, textiles or toys from the era of your own childhood, and with second-hand furniture, you don't have to worry about wear and tear. You should be aware of safety issues, though, ensuring that all pieces are sufficiently robust, and – if your children are young – can't be taken apart. Never buy a vintage cot, however lovely it looks, because it won't comply with modern safety standards. If you're desperate for a nostalgic nursery, choose a wood-and-metal reproduction crib, while painted sleigh beds, mahogany lits bateaux and iron four-posters are all fun for older children, and are often as inexpensive as the

high-street versions. If you have older children, you could encourage them to source and buy their own "cool" vintage furniture, from a 50s metal desk to a tatty chest of drawers from a thrift shop that they can paint in whatever colour they choose.

You can also work period textiles and bedding into a scheme for a child's room. Hunt out vintage material from the 50s, 60s or 70s, with whimsical designs or classic character prints, and sew into cushion covers, stretch over an artist's canvas to make a wall hanging, or use to upholster the seat of a desk chair. Another option is to look out for original film posters and book illustrations and frame them to put on the wall. For a nursery, it's also fun to collect vintage letters, from old printers' blocks to metal shop-fascia letters, and use them to gradually amass an alphabet wall. By all means collect and display vintage toys, too, but for safety's sake, keep them on a high shelf.

BATHROOMS

BELOW LEFT When it comes to choosing sanitaryware, think outside the box. A sink with an integral draining board, salvaged from a kitchen, can be given a new lease on life in a simple bathroom, with built-in cupboards beneath.

BELOW RIGHT In a 20th-century house, it is appropriate to use modestly proportioned basins, chrome taps and lighting common to the era. This bathroom, originally built in the 30s, retains all its original features.

The vogue for modern, almost clinical, bathrooms is now very widespread, but including some salvage sanitaryware in your bathroom will give you a truly unique look. On top of that, you'll be getting fantastic quality. Think of putting together a creative combination of individual pieces, rather than a matching suite and although pieces in pale yellow, pink, grey or blue come up occasionally, most sanitaryware is white. This makes a mix-and-match approach easier to achieve.

Take time to research where to buy and decide on your price point. It's usually best to get vintage bathroom fittings from a reputable salvage yard, rather than picking up items from skips. Dealers usually have a wide selection of fittings and some specialise only in bathrooms. A good dealer will ensure second-hand goods are fully restored and will work with 21st-century plumbing. When buying a reconditioned piece, find out if it's guaranteed and

Soften an urban vintage look by choosing pieces with gentle curves. In this New York bathroom, the drape of the shower curtain and the rounded contours of the roll-top bath and basin balance the angular industrial-style windows.

THIS PAGE If you love the look of old-fashioned taps, but don't want to faithfully reproduce a retro bathroom, then mix and match. Here, a cast concrete basin looks elegant teamed with mosaic tiles and vintage taps.

if so for how long. If you're buying "as seen", for instance at an auction, check carefully for cracks, stains, stiff taps and rust.

VINTAGE BATHS, BASINS, WCs AND TAPS

Think of an old bath, and it's often the cast-iron roll-top baths that come to mind. But there's a wide choice of materials, including tin, copper, marble, ceramic, and earthenware, as well as a range of styles — deep double-ended metal bateau bathtubs, which can look very contemporary when teamed with modern architecture, coloured ceramic Art Deco baths with a moulded "skirt", the slipper bath, with one end higher

than the other, and the canopy bath, incorporating a built-in shower screen and shower rose.

As well as shape, consider finish. A good dealer will re-enamel the inside of the bath, but think about the exterior too. Cast-iron baths can often be repainted or given a polished or patinated metal exterior.

Most old basins are in the traditional pedestal style, but you can also find wall-hung basins on brackets or legs, as well as those that incorporate a splashback. Some French basins, such as those in fine porcelain with gently rounded contours on tapered legs, are particularly elegant. For a simple country look, a plain English pedestal basin is appropriate, and for an

THIS PAGE We may think of the mixer tap as a modern invention, but it's also possible to buy mixer taps in traditional styles. Set into a sleek marble worktop, these pretty little taps add extra character to a simple bathroom.

industrial bathroom, consider a quirky basin, perhaps salvaged from a public washroom or a 20s hairdresser's basin. Simple basins with fancy cast-iron brackets or a vintage corner basin are other options.

It's comparatively rare to find an original old WC so most of us will have to be content to team a new toilet with vintage pieces or add a salvaged mahogany Victorian toilet seat to a modern WC. As a rule of thumb, pick a high-level cistern for a late 19th- or early 20th-century mood, low-level for a 20th-century look. Cisterns were often beautifully made, and came with ribbed, floral-printed or prettily shaped designs. You might even find a vintage French bidet.

When you're choosing old taps, keep the practicalities firmly in mind and ensure that they have been cleaned and fitted with new washers so they work without any stiffness or leaks. Fittings should have been converted to suit modern plumbing sizes and you

should also consider the reach of the spout as old taps didn't conform to a standard size. Think, too, about the finish. Most old taps are brass but they can often be re-plated in nickel or chrome, which would be more appropriate with 20th-century bathroom styles.

Styles vary enormously, from squared-off Art Deco designs to hospital-style lever taps, and from traditional early 20th-century bath/shower mixer taps, to very plain pillar taps. For a modern vintage bathroom, try contrasting old taps with contemporary sanitaryware.

REPRODUCTION SANITARYWARE
If you're nervous about using salvaged fittings, opt for a reproduction. Or, if you have found one amazing vintage buy, but can't find other old fittings to match, mix reproduction with the real thing. The range of styles varies from a pretty Art Nouveau washstand with cabriole legs, to a perfect copy of a Victorian shower

OPPOSITE FAR LEFT The traditional, popular cast-iron roll top bath has many guises, according to the way it is accessorised. For a grand vintage boudoir look, team one with elaborate legs, wall-mounted taps and a marble-effect floor and walls.

LEFT Half the fun of putting together a vintage bathroom lies in putting together the unexpected. Here, a decorated copper slipper bath is accompanied by Roman-style paint effects and by a bold, brass water spout.

THIS PAGE Although this is a modern bathroom, it has a distinctive retro mood. These design echoes come from the grey and yellow tiles, whose colours are reminiscent of 30s bathrooms, as well as from the plainness of the tiles – also typical of the era.

canopy or a French bow-fronted basin on a nickel-plated frame. Such copies are rarely cheap, but they certainly deliver the vintage look.

CUSTOMISING

For a more relaxed mix-and-match vintage mood, then you need to think creatively when you're out shopping. By putting individual elements together in a new way, you can save money and have a more individual look. For example, antique roll-top baths often come without legs, so why not stand one on chunky wooden blocks? Or team an old marble wash-stand with a modern countertop basin and wall-mounted spout. Or, if you have found a perfect 20s coloured basin with

a broken pedestal, have a pair of brackets made by your local metalwork company and mount it on the wall.

Similarly, if you have a plain white bathroom suite that you can't change, add salvaged taps for a quirkier effect. Or you could panel a simple white bath with mirror for a glamorous Art Deco look, or hang a giant foxed-glass antique mirror above a basin.

WALLS AND FLOORS

Modern tiles and surfaces make a great contrast with vintage sanitaryware. For example, a metal slipper bath or ceramic French basin gets a modern twist when teamed with mosaic tiles in white or black, with a wall of brightly coloured painted glass, or with a stainless-

OPPOSITE BELOW LEFT
It's not essential to choose country-style sanitaryware for a rustic property. Play with contrasts. Here, the surprise choice of this charming double washstand with elegant legs works well because it is carefully accessorised with rustic stools.

OPPOSITE BELOW RIGHT
If you're going for a specific period look, as in this funky 70s bathroom, pay attention to getting the details right. Here, the

style is set as much by the period-perfect floor and ceiling treatments, colour scheme and furniture, as by the sanitaryware.

BELOW RIGHT For an unusual decorative twist, customise a vintage piece of furniture to create a vanity unit. Here, a traditional old table with turned legs is paired with a new stainless-steel washbasin, to offer a pleasing mix of retro and modern style.

Great items to invest in include old galvanized metal medicine cabinets or pretty glass-and-chrome 30s cabinets. A trolley is useful for holding bottles and jars; try an ex-factory trolley for an industrial vintage look. Mirrors are also good buys; they range from gilded and gently flaking styles that are perfect for the boudoir mood, to giant panelled mirrors from hotels that double the sense of space in a small bathroom.

Also look out for incidental extras – a decorative Victorian cast-iron lavatory roll holder or an old shaving mirror on an extending arm. And if you're time poor but still want the vintage bathroom look, then you can cheat. There are plenty of websites devoted to selling authentic copies of beautiful old accessories.

steel floor. Glass bricks make a dramatic background to colourful 20s sanitaryware. In a boudoir-style vintage bathroom, choose a modern wallpaper with large-scale leaves or flowers, while in a seaside bathroom, pale grey-blue tongue-and-groove wall panelling is smart with plain white Edwardian fittings.

If you want to keep to a period mood, then plain brick-shaped metro tiles in white, black or green are classics, and will look as good with a roll-top bath and pedestal washbasin as with an Art Deco suite. For a 30s mood, add a black-and-white chequerboard border. Lino is an enduring choice for floors, while marble looks sophisticated with a bateau or slipper bath. If your heart is set on marble but your budget won't stretch to a large expanse, then consider using a piece to top a vanity unit and add a small marble splashback.

ACCESSORIES
Whether you want to further enhance period fittings or stamp a gentle vintage mood onto a plain white bathroom, accessories will make all the difference.

Vintage Elements

We all know that it is the furniture, textiles and decorative objects in a home that truly crystallise a particular interior look. Whether you choose to mimic a certain decade or loosely interpret a vintage style, it makes sense to do your homework on key designers, prevalent trends and even the social movements of a given period. This will not only help you achieve the effect you want, but will mean it's easier to haggle with dealers and traders if you know what is, or isn't, a good example of a key vintage look.

Once you have settled on a particular vintage style and have started putting a room together, hone the key details, beginning with the hardware. Though this may be small in scale — such as light switches and doorknobs — picking good copies or distressed originals will really help to link your larger retro buys with your home's architecture, even when that architecture is modern.

When choosing furniture, take time not only to look at the style, but also at the construction, materials, even the furniture maker's stamp if there is one. The same care should go into choosing fabrics, ceramics, glass and pictures, but don't get too carried away. Putting together a vintage style isn't just about getting design history right, but is also about the decorative mood. So try to choose nostalgic, quirky and original pieces that please your eye, for that is what will ultimately add character to your vintage home.

OPPOSITE ABOVE LEFT Radiators take up space so they have a big visual impact. Reconditioned radiators can be plain or decorative styles, and come in many shapes.

OPPOSITE ABOVE RIGHT Choosing furniture with the right silhouette, finish, size and shape is key. This rustic cupboard combines good looks and practicality.

OPPOSITE CENTRE LEFT Take time to identify key looks and styles. In the 50s, designers experimented with fluid, organic shapes, especially for coffee tables.

OPPOSITE CENTRE RIGHT Original period light fittings aren't the only option. You can find new fittings made from recycled objects.

OPPOSITE BELOW LEFT Many 20th-century chairs, such as this PK9, have become iconic objects in their own right.

OPPOSITE BELOW RIGHT Starting a collection of small decorative objects, from china to paintings, is a simple way to ease into vintage style. Buy just one piece at a time, to get a feel for what attracts you.

ABOVE Original salvaged hooks are often no more expensive than modern copies. Here, a rustic wooden peg rail suits a country vintage interior; robust steel hooks are good for urban interiors; brass and porcelain coat hooks suit a glamorous boudoir style.

OPPOSITE The finish of a reconditioned radiator is just as crucial as the shape. Most salvage yards will sandblast, prime and paint in a colour of your choice, or will polish the original cast iron for an industrial finish.

HARDWARE

It is often the small items such as hardware that can actively help to stamp a vintage style on a home. Details like radiators, door knobs and hooks can be hard to get excited about, but the eye still registers them and modern equivalents may jar with period furniture.

If you have the money, swapping modern radiators for cast-iron originals is worth it. Yes, they cost almost as much as a piece of furniture, but radiators are very visible, so it pays to get them right and there are plenty to choose from. It's a good idea to source them fully restored from a salvage dealer who can offer at least a one-year guarantee. Generally, a restored radiator should have had its old valves removed and should then have been sandblasted back to the bare iron, pressure-tested, primed and painted. For a gritty, urban vintage look, ask to have the cast-iron burnished to a highly polished finish.

Old radiators are generally priced by the section, and come in many shapes and sizes, including rare circular versions. For a pretty boudoir mood, look for an ornately patterned radiator. You can also find Victorian and Edwardian cast-iron radiator covers.

Door furniture can also set the appropriate vintage tone. Although many hardware companies offer excellent period reproductions, it's fun to hunt out the real thing. If you are refurbishing an entire house, it's always worth asking a salvage dealer if a particular style is available in quantity. However, using similar styles can look good, too. Most 19th-century door knobs were made in cast iron or brass, but as the 20th century dawned, nickel and chrome plating became more common and ceramic, wood and crystal door knobs also grew in popularity. Pick a style that feels right with the architecture of your home: square chrome Art Deco door knobs are ideal in a 30s house, whereas more decorative brass knobs suit a Victorian house with panelled doors.

It's also satisfying to search salvage dealers and vintage websites for old coat hooks, cupboard pull handles and front door knockers. Old hardware was often beautifully made and a one-off design will add character. For a country vintage look, stick to simple metal or wood designs, but for a more decorative finish, you can find examples in elaborate brass and ceramic, sometimes bearing flowers or leaves. And if you want to add a subtle period finish to new cupboard doors, small vintage brass, crystal, porcelain or cast-iron knobs are perfect.

FURNITURE

Furniture has such a strong decorative influence on the look of your home, that you should be sure to choose it carefully. For the most relaxed, naturally evolved effect, vintage style offers the opportunity to mix pieces from different periods with a selection of modern buys.

Until the late 19th century, all chairs were handmade from wood. Choose according to your vintage style: a simple early 19th-century fruitwood chair, say, for a country vintage look, or a gilded 18th-century Louis XV-style chair for vintage boudoir. Mass-production came later in the century, starting with Michael Thonet's now classic bentwood chair, but the Arts and Crafts movement brought a return to the hand-crafted aesthetic.

In the 20th century, furniture designers and architects focussed increasingly on the chair and new materials. Some iconic examples of the 20s include Marcel Breuer's Wassily chair and Mies van der Rohe's Barcelona

BELOW LEFT An iconic chair looks different according to its surroundings. The organic lines of Arne Jacobsen's Bull chair are particularly striking in this drawing room, where they are contrasted with traditional architecture and classical proportions.

BELOW RIGHT To show off a chair with fluid lines, juxtapose it against contrasting silhouettes. In this London flat, the swoop of the armchair stands out against the square contours of a seating cube and a contemporary fire surround.

ABOVE LEFT The low-slung, upholstered wood-framed armchair became popular in the 50s as post-war furniture designers moved away from the heavy three-piece suites of the early 20th century.

ABOVE RIGHT The Cherner chair was a classic design of the 50s, and versions are still made today according to the original specifications. Its graceful arms are a distinguishing feature.

RIGHT Take time to delve into the date and origins of a particular chair's design, as it makes buying more interesting. The Antony chair, designed in 1950 by Jean Prouvé, was originally intended for commercial use.

THIS PAGE After the 50s, the chunky sofa returned to favour, either in amorphous shapes or in modular configurations. This classic segmented design, originally created by DeSede in the 70s, gives the room a wonderfully retro feel.

OPPOSITE In this New York apartment, the mood is Pop Art 60s, but the furniture is contemporary and custom-made. A good furniture maker should be able to copy a particularly appealing retro design.

chair. In the 30s came laminated wood, as used by Alvar Aalto for his famous birch stacking stool, while after World War II, Charles and Ray Eames produced chairs like the LCW in moulded and bent birch-faced plywood and the innovative DAR in fibreglass, steel and rubber. Any of these would sit happily in an urban vintage open-plan sitting room or to add a retro mood in a modern kitchen/dining room.

The 50s – regarded by some as the heyday of 20th-century furniture – brought chairs in fluid shapes that could easily be moved around people's increasingly open-plan living spaces. Key designs of the era include Harry Bertoia's Diamond chair and Arne Jacobsen's Series 7 chair. Original designer chairs will be costly, but many others of that era have a similar feel and a less expensive price tag.

By the late 50s and 60s, experimentation with plastics was all the rage, leading to classic designs like

ABOVE Twentieth-century furniture designers have come up with some elegant variations on the traditional chaise longue. The PK24, designed in 1965 by Poul Kjærholm, is made in woven cane and stainless steel. It is both comfortable and attractive.

ABOVE LEFT Comfort and practicality should play a part in sofa-buying decisions. The trusty Victorian sofa was often beautifully made and well-proportioned, so it makes a classic and reliable choice for a family sitting room.

OPPOSITE Sofas from the latter part of the 20th century have a tendency to appear lumpy, so break up the look by combining them with elegant chairs. Here, a dark leather sofa is balanced with a classic white Barcelona armchair.

THERE'S A REASON WHY
ICONIC PIECES OF
FURNITURE REMAIN
POPULAR. THESE CLASSICS
COMBINE ELEGANCE OF LINE
AND COMFORT WITH A
NOSTALGIC NOD TO THE
RECENT PAST.

Verner Panton's curvy polypropylene Panton chair and Robin Day's Polyprop chair. In the 70s, some designers were drawn to increasingly avant-garde designs, but companies such as G-Plan opted for inexpensive mass-produced furniture. Any of these late 20th-century styles would work well for a retro vintage look.

SOFAS AND CHAISE LONGUES
Your chosen vintage style will influence your choice of sofa, too. For those in search of a shabby-chic or country vintage look, then Victorian buttoned Chesterfield sofas or traditional chaise longues are perfect. For a more urban vintage style or for retro vintage, you might opt for a curvy – but bulky – wood-trimmed leather Art Deco sofa, a lighter looking teak-armed upholstered 50s sofa, or a 60s or 70s space-age or Pop Art-influenced colourful sofa with an unusual serpentine shape and curvy silhouette.

Generally speaking, the earlier the piece, the more bulky it will be, which, together with your style choice, might be a factor in your decision-making.

TABLES
Vintage tables also reflect experimentation by furniture designers and architects, changing tastes and methods of production. An ornately carved mahogany Victorian dining table would be perfect in a smart city flat, perhaps softened with antique linen-upholstered dining chairs, while a bird's eye maple or walnut Art Nouveau or Art Deco side table, with their leaner lines and organic styling, would look chic in a vintage boudoir bedroom.

Utility furniture from World War II was well made from solid wood – often oak or mahogany. Strong, serviceable kitchen or dining tables are perfect for today's small living spaces and look funky teamed with modern moulded plastic chairs.

Post-war, designers experimented with tapered wooden legs, light steel tubular frames, and used new tabletop materials such as laminate, plywood and glass. Perhaps the most famous example is Eero Saarinen's iconic Tulip pedestal table for Knoll.

If you can't afford a true design classic, then look for originals from firms like Heals, Habitat and G-Plan, all of which produced inexpensive but well designed tables in lighter woods like pine, maple and beech.

The coffee table is a 20th-century invention, but there are pretty examples of side tables from the early 20s onwards. Eileen Gray's classic adjustable side table has a restrained look, while Art Deco and 30s mirrored side tables (and cocktail cabinets), are perfect for vintage boudoir. The organic shapes of 50s coffee tables, often with laminate, teak or glass tops, and sometimes integral magazines racks, too, are perfect for an urban or retro vintage room, as is a 70s nest of tables in light wood or in smoked glass and tubular steel.

THIS PAGE The classic butler's tray table is endlessly adaptable. It's perfect for serving drinks in a sitting room or as an extra side table in a dining room, and it's robust enough for kitchen use.

OPPOSITE ABOVE This design-classic dining table takes centre-stage even when it's not in use. In this 60s-style American apartment, a collection of red glass adds drama.

OPPOSITE BELOW LEFT The ever-popular 50s Tulip table, designed by Eero Saarinen, looks at home in a 20th-century apartment. Here it stands in a Pennsylvanian farmhouse, teamed with 19th-century French country chairs.

OPPOSITE BELOW RIGHT It is often easy to find side tables at reasonable prices, and they add much more charm than a modern mass-produced version. Teamed with a chic little slipper chair, this decorative table doubles as a drinks table.

THIS PAGE It isn't cheating to use re-issues of classic vintage furniture, so long as they are manufactured according to the original specifications. In this 50s house, re-issues of a George Nelson sofa and coffee table appear to be totally authentic.

OPPOSITE The joy of mixing together vintage pieces is that it is positively acceptable to break the rules. In this enterprising combination, classic Arne Jacobsen Series 7 chairs have been teamed with a rustic French antique table.

MIRRORS

Antique mirrors can be expensive, but many 19th- and 20th-century examples are affordable. Some frames were gilded, and mirrors whose gilt has flaked off are particularly appropriate for the vintage mood. For a glittery boudoir look, choose a sparkly Venetian mirror; for country vintage, go for a distressed painted, or simple wood-framed style from the Arts and Crafts or Edwardian era. If you're lucky enough to find a funky space-age-influenced 60s or 70s mirror, it will look great in a retro room, while a quirkily shaped 30s mirror with bevelled-glass edges, or a Hollywood-inspired Art Deco mirror add vintage glamour to a contemporary space.

ABOVE If other pieces of furniture are elaborate, keep to a simpler mirror style. Seek out distressed hand-painted or gilded frames, and foxed glass with soft blemishes, which is much more interesting than too-perfect new glass.

RIGHT A mirror is both a piece of furniture and a wall decoration, so when you are hanging it, ensure that it sits well for both. In this symmetrically arranged room, a plain mirror works particularly well.

OPPOSITE A gilded 19th-century French mirror is a classic choice and is well worth the investment. Less is always more: in this modest hallway, a giant decorative mirror brings plenty of drama without the need for other major pieces.

Caring for vintage leather

- If the seat of a leather armchair is worn, instead of reupholstering the entire piece, get a specialist upholsterer to create a new feather-filled seat pad.

- An antique dealer or leather specialist should be able to source antique leather to create as close a match as possible for new pads.

- Re-colour tiny scratches on old leather using a matching shoe polish, and stitch up any small tears.

Leather is a traditional favourite for upholstering chairs, sofas and daybeds, whether Victorian buttoned Chesterfields or comfortable Edwardian club armchairs. The worn patina of the leather is part of its enduring appeal. Tired leather upholstery should be regularly cleaned with saddle soap and gently buffed with a soft cloth. Use a specialist cleaner for small stains: some leather specialists offer antique repair kits that include leather colourants for touching up damage. Never use water and detergent. For water spillages, immediately soak up the water with kitchen paper towel; to treat new grease stains, sprinkle on talcum powder. Always keep old leather furniture away from a direct heat source, such as radiators, or the leather will crack even more.

ABOVE AND RIGHT Tan and black are classic leather shades, used in all eras, but look out for the reds, yellows, greens and blues of the 50s and 60s.

OPPOSITE This leather club armchair is a genuine classic, that looks at home in a gritty urban interior but is also perfect for a vintage country look.

LIGHTING

Whether you invest in a dramatic chandelier or a pair of discreet table lamps, the lighting styles you pick will directly influence the final look of each room. We're all encouraged to use lighting as a tool to improve ambience. In the vintage home, the best choices combine stylish period looks with a good balance of overhead, side and task lighting. When you have found your vintage light fitting, it may well need re-wiring for 21st-century use. That job, as well as cleaning and repairing, is best left to the professionals.

CHANDELIERS AND PENDANT LIGHTS

Most vintage chandeliers were either designed to hold candles or, if from the latter part of the 19th century, oil lamps. If you're looking for a dainty style, perhaps for a bedroom, avoid the large Victorian designs, and opt for pretty little 20s versions or kitsch interpretations from the 50s.

BELOW In a modern space, experiment with a bold light fitting. This one, by David Weeks, is in the spirit of Serge Mouille's classic mid-20th-century lighting designs.

BELOW LEFT An antique chandelier imparts instant vintage charm, but its scale must be correct. In this grand drawing room, with strong classical proportions, a tiny chandelier would have looked lost.

THIS PAGE Funky 60s and 70s pendant light fittings often feature frosted glass and unusual silhouettes. Vintage dealers frequently offer lights for sale as collectors' items. If that's the case with the light you buy, always have it checked by an electrician to make sure it's safe to use.

As the 20th century progressed, the central pendant light superseded the chandelier. For an Art Nouveau or Art Deco mood, look out for the characteristic moulded white or pale pastel glass lampshades of the period. These pretty glass shades shouldn't cost a fortune. After World War II, the Scandinavians produced some of the classic styles of the era: in particular the PH-5 lamp, designed by Poul Henningsen and Arne Jacobsen's dome-shaped AJ lamp. These remain classic choices today for the retro vintage fan.

In the 60s and 70s – apart from Ingo Maurer's one-off, and now iconic Bulb design – pendant lamp choices tended either towards organic silhouettes or reflected the Space-Age fascination of the era. Spiky, Sputnik-style chandeliers in glass and chrome, or chandeliers featuring cubes of frosted or coloured glass were popular. If you're after a simpler, urban vintage mood,

A PENDANT LIGHT DOMINATES THE EYE-LINE SO CHOOSE A BOLD, SCALED-UP SHAPE TO SET THE DECORATIVE TONE, FROM RETRO ORGANIC TO CHUNKY INDUSTRIAL.

OPPOSITE LEFT Pleated plastic pendant lights are particularly representative of the 70s, especially after Poul Christiansen designed his iconic Le Klint light in 1971, made from a single sheet of folded plastic.

OPPOSITE RIGHT Ex-factory pendant light fittings, mainly in coloured enamel, are a wonderful choice for hanging above a dining table or kitchen island unit. You can aso buy new versions in a similar retro style.

ABOVE Vintage lighting dealers are excellent sources of unusual spotlights. Old lights from photographic studios, or marine or factory spotlights look funky. They are available in re-polished metal or the original distressed finish.

ABOVE RIGHT Lighting designs featuring metal shades in orb, cone or cylinder shapes were popular from the 50s onwards. Look for floor lights with adjustable arms, to create a dramatic silhouette as well as excellent ambient lighting.

look out for giant ex-factory enamel pendant shades, or use retro abstract-print fabrics to create simple, drum-shaped pendant lampshades that you can arrange so they hang low over a dining table or an armchair.

STANDARD AND SIDE LIGHTS

The right choice of standard lamp can imprint a particularly strong vintage stamp on a room. A traditional Edwardian turned wooden lamp base teamed with a silk, tassel-edged shade, perfectly suits a country vintage sitting room. Both of these can easily be found at car boot sales or junk shops. Exotic chrome standard lamps with glass globe shades, or bases in unusual woods like walnut, were popular during the Art Deco period, and suit a vintage boudoir look. As the 20th century progressed, standard lamps took on a cleaner-cut silhouette. One of the most enduring styles

is the classic Bestlite BL3, or 30 years later, the Arco floor lamp by Achille and Pier Castiglioni. This lamp introduced a fluid, modern sweep that was in tune with the organic shapes popular at the time. Originally designed to illuminate a dining table, it was, and is still, more commonly used as a floor lamp.

Vintage side lights can be comparatively inexpensive and are a great way of introducing the feel of a particular period into a room. Art Deco side lights in chrome and clear or frosted glass look extremely glamorous, while the angular, flowerpot-shaped lampshades of the 50s have a simpler, more clean-cut feel that would suit a retro vintage interior. For a dash of retro vintage in a funky living room, you can't beat the classic lava lamp, which first appeared in 1963 but which is now back in production and selling worldwide.

THIS PAGE For elegant side lighting, look for period table lamps with ceramic, Murano glass or découpage bases. Choose bright colours for a modern interior, muted shades for a vintage boudoir look. Team with a plain lampshade.

OPPOSITE ABOVE Mushroom-shaped side lamps became popular in the late 60s and 70s. They were often available in bright pop art colours like red or orange, as well as in monochrome shades.

OPPOSITE BELOW LEFT With its telescopic stem and arched silhouette, the Arco light, designed in 1962 by Achille and Pier Castiglioni, remains a 20th-century classic. This floor lamp will grace any sitting room with a retro vintage look.

OPPOSITE BELOW RIGHT The trusty standard lamp, teamed with a plain drum lampshade, not only provides excellent mood lighting, but adds a retro feel to a sitting room.

RIGHT Industrial-style lighting on extending arms or flexible brackets, makes excellent task lighting. Examples from as early as the 30s, like this one, look surprisingly modern today. Choose polished steel for sophistication, un-restored metal for a grittier look.

BELOW As the 70s progressed task lights became smaller and leaner. Now considered a classic, Richard Sapper's Tizio light, designed in 1972, was one of the forerunners of today's streamlined desk lighting.

OPPOSITE Classic styles, such as this 50s articulated wall light in polished metal by French manufacturer Jieldé , look simple enough to use in a kitchen. But for bedroom use, look out for unusually decorative variations, with glass or shell-shaped metal shades.

TASK LIGHTS

The most iconic task light of all time is the Anglepoise lamp, patented in 1932, and in production for over 50 years. Nothing beats its engineering and simple good looks, and it's still possible to pick up originals in a variety of colours. If the paint is slightly scratched, so much the better. They really suit the industrial vintage look. More serious retro vintage collectors should look out for lamps by Modernist designers such as Eileen Gray, Christian Dell and Marianne Brandt, all of whom created beautiful – and now highly collectible – task lights in simple, yet functional shapes throughout the 30s. For a 60s or 70s mood, look out for reading lamps in Pop-Art colours, and in organic silhouettes: mushroom shapes were especially popular.

SOFT FURNISHINGS

Finding attractive vintage textiles is no easy task. Specialist vintage textile websites, shops and dealers offer the best choice, but you can also visit antique textile fairs. Some vintage dealers offer a wide selection, from Victorian to the 70s, while others specialise in the mid- to late 20th-century. Yet others only deal in named designer textiles, which fetch higher prices, while a few offer modern furnishing fabrics that use authentic 20th-century designs. Then there are those dealers who sell fabric on the roll, while others have smaller pieces – for instance, the original manufacturer's fabric samples – and yet others specialise in vintage curtains or blinds.

In a different category are the vintage fabric dealers who specialise in rustic continental textiles, from antique French linen sheets and tablecloths, to hand-loomed country linens, recycled grain sacks, tea towels and monogrammed fabric pieces. These dealers sometimes make these textiles up into new accessories such as cushions or lampshades. And the final source of vintage textiles is perhaps the most fun – hunting out examples yourself, in junk shops, at car boot sales, or even on eBay.

You should buy with care, though. Particularly if you're purchasing from a website, read the descriptions and look at the photographs. Though it's great to find fabrics offered in mint condition, remember that the occasional hole or stain can be cut around, disguised with appliqué or gently darned. And while it's fine to machine-wash linen, more delicate fabrics like silk, embroidery, or even cotton, will need to be hand-washed or dry-cleaned. Precious details, like horn or wood buttons, or lace, also require extra care.

CHOICE OF FABRIC

Choose fabrics according to the style you want: rough-textured antique linens, sometimes with a colourful stripe, are perfect for simple country or coastal vintage looks, as are pretty vegetable-dyed pieces. Faded floral cottons and embroidered linens suit simple shabby chic vintage interiors. Look for 30s cotton or linen furnishing fabrics featuring tiny floral motifs, or 40s leaf prints, or prints of roses in full bloom. Delicate floral 19th-century and Art Nouveau fabrics look demure in a boudoir setting, while streamlined, graphic Art Deco prints are especially appropriate teamed with mirrored furniture.

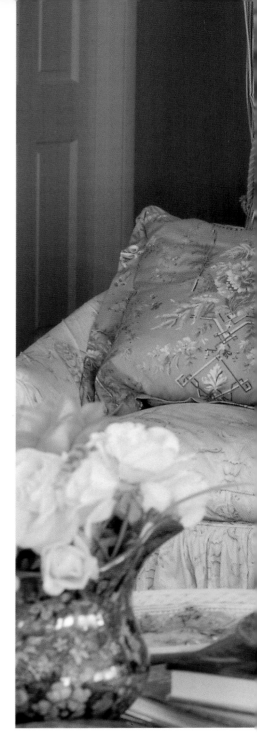

CURTAINS AND BLINDS

Going down the vintage textile route means choosing between making new curtains or blinds out of vintage fabric, or customising second-hand finds. If you have enough vintage fabric, you can use it to make curtains in an appropriate style. Stitch 30s chintz, for example, into generously gathered curtains teamed with a flat or frilled pelmet, or make a funky graphic 50s print into a plain roller blind or gathered pelmet-free curtains.

If you only have a small piece of fabric, try using it as a panel, surrounded by borders of contrasting plain modern fabric. Alternatively, stitch together several pieces of vintage ribbon into a band that will give a curtain the necessary extra length. Smaller pieces of textile, from antique grain sacks to monogrammed damask napkins, make pretty little roller or Roman blinds, neither of which need much fabric.

The post-war mood of the 50s was for vibrant colour and abstract patterns and this decade saw an explosion of interest in textile design. These are the fabrics to choose for a retro vintage mood. Although the key designer of the period was Lucienne Day, whose whimsical, abstract designs are instantly recognisable and now fetch high prices, there are plenty of 50s textiles by unnamed designers that you can find at far lower prices. Look out for whimsical designs: anything from sketchy deckchair prints to cars, aeroplanes and fruit-and-vegetable kitchen motifs. In the 60s, when Pop Art and flower power were at their height, fabrics were designed with everything from monochrome black and white spots and stripes, to large abstract florals and psychedelic paisleys. Then along came the 70s, when a combination of brown and orange was the colour scheme of choice, with graphic swirls and flower prints being the most popular motifs.

THIS PAGE Customising precious old textiles, whether a shawl or a remnant of antique material, is often the way forward. This curtain was created by stitching together half a length of silk sari, and a section of plain material.

OPPOSITE ABOVE Sheer vintage textiles, such as lace or fine linen, make a pretty choice for privacy blinds, especially if teamed with classic wooden shutters. Use the fabric unlined: a plain panel or simple roll-up blind works best.

OPPOSITE BELOW If you have sufficient second-hand fabric to make up into full-length curtains – and if the pattern is particularly attractive – then choose a plain style to show off the vintage motifs and colours to best advantage.

OPPOSITE Although often associated with less than stylish Victoriana, patchwork can look very modern. It is also a brilliant way of using scraps of vintage material to create new full-length curtains, bedcovers or blinds .

ABOVE Pieces of lace, old cutwork embroidered bed sheets, even antique tablecloths, can all be cut to size and hung as dress curtains for a decorative boudoir mood. These drapes framing a doorway feature fringed lace used to create a delicate pelmet.

THIS PAGE Scatter cushions are a wonderful way to introduce small pieces of vintage fabric into a room. For a mid 20th-century mood, choose abstract designs and keep the cushion shape plain. These 50s screen-printed linen cushion covers are Scandinavian.

RIGHT Choosing to use second-hand textiles isn't just about finding patterned material from a particular era. For those who prefer plains, concentrate on texture: fabrics soften beautifully with age, so look out for vintage linens, cottons or silk and mix them together.

BELOW Not all antique fabrics need to be sourced close to home. Look out for old pieces of embroidered silks from the Far East – this chaise longue features gold cushions and Burmese blankets – to create a decorative exotic look.

CUSHIONS

Cushion covers use up small scraps or offcuts of vintage textiles, or even vintage silk scarves. Mount extremely small panels on a larger piece of fabric or seek out antique linen specialists who make new cushions to order using old monogrammed pieces as the central panel – perfect for a country vintage interior.

When making cushion covers, you don't have to stick to square shapes: long, thin rectangular cushions, bolsters and round cushions are interesting variants, as are – for a 70s retro room – giant floor cushions. Enjoy mixing and matching fabrics, but keep to a theme. For example, in a vintage boudoir, a chaise longue looks pretty piled with cushions in flower-embroidered silks, while in a retro vintage room, a 50s sofa is enhanced with cushions in different graphic prints of the era, but all one colour – blue or brown, for example. And finally, don't overstuff the cushions: somehow vintage fabrics encasing floppy cushions look best.

- Reupholstering in a smart new dark fabric like wool, linen or chenille highlights a prettily shaped chair and makes a dramatic contrast to a gilded wood frame.

- Bring a chair up to date with antique linen sheeting. An old linen grain sack is a good choice if only the seat needs to be recovered.

- Use contrast colour piping or buttoning, decorative upholstery nails, or new trimmings to dress up a reupholstered vintage chair.

Reupholstering chairs

When you are tempted to buy a vintage armchair, it's best to assume it will need to be reupholstered, so bear this in mind when you're calculating if you have found a bargain. To tell if a chair needs to be reupholstered, run your hand under the base. If the webbing is slack or the springs aren't upright, it's a sure sign that reupholstery will be required. Alternatively, sit in the chair: if you sink too low, the webbing has given way. Having a chair reupholstered gives you the opportunity to get the wooden frame re-jointed and checked for woodworm, which can be treated if necessary. If you find a chair with wooden arms and legs and an upholstered seat and back, don't be tempted to over-restore – gently flaking paint or gilding will add to its vintage appeal.

ABOVE Good quality, classic fabrics like wool, velvet and tapestry wear well, so it's not always necessary to re-upholster.

OPPOSITE AND RIGHT When revamping a wood-framed chair, choose a neutral fabric to echo the soft tones of a pale distressed frame, and a dark fabric for a bold contrast with gilded wood.

DECORATIVE ACCESSORIES

Decorative accessories offer a wonderfully individual way of finishing off our homes. Eclectic collectors may want a massed display, while for others, a few perfectly chosen objects is the ultimate aim. With vintage style, the fun lies in mixing vintage with what you already possess.

PAINTINGS AND PHOTOS

Any style of image goes in the vintage home. If your taste is traditional, buy inexpensive Victorian watercolours or prints with a theme such as dogs or landscapes. If you like 20th-century art but can't afford the big names, identify a favourite 20th-century art movement and find works by lesser-known artists.

Black-and-white photographs are a less expensive alternative and can be found on specialist websites. There's everything from architecture and portraits, to still lifes and film. Fashion and book illustrations, or film posters, bristle with period details, and can stamp a room with a strong vintage mood.

ABOVE Entire walls covered with treasures look dramatic. Choose one or more unifying devices. Here, the brightly coloured walls draw the disparate objects together: while one wall features butterfly collections, the other displays the owner's own artwork.

ABOVE LEFT It's essential to plan a proper display for a mismatched collection of framed prints, paintings and photographs, otherwise everything looks muddled. This apparently casual arrangement has in fact been artfully arranged on narrow shelves.

THIS PAGE If the aim is to show off a themed collection, it's helpful to pay attention to details. This display of fashion drawings and photographs appears relaxed, but the colours and tones are deliberately similar.

THIS PAGE A display of coloured glass needs to have light and space around it. Here every piece of glass is different in terms of period, style and shape, but the arrangement works because the colours hang together tonally.

OPPOSITE There is a powerful appeal in showing off china en masse, and the beauty lies in the similarity of colour and design. This collection of creamware, from shell dishes to sauce boats, has been symmetrically arranged for maximum impact.

GLASS AND CERAMICS

Collecting glass and ceramics can be as simple as choosing a theme or colour and adding to it each time you visit a junk shop. Some collections won't cost a fortune. For example, you can pick up inexpensive oddments of Georgian or Victorian glassware, while 20th-century glass offers rich pickings. Art Nouveau and Art Deco are always popular and 50s Scandinavian modern studio glass is very collectible, as is some later glass, such as the funky Handkerchief vases.

Period china is always popular, while 20th-century ceramics include costly pieces by named 20s and 30s designers like Clarice Cliff and Susie Cooper. Less expensive finds might include Art Deco dinner services, 50s and 60s pieces by Portmeirion, Denby, Hornsea, Midwinter and Poole Pottery or Scandinavian ceramics of the 50s to the 70s, which are also very collectible.

LARGER DECORATIVE OBJECTS

Many vintage websites and reclamation yards offer eccentric, outsized or frankly strange items. These can add immense character to a room. A tiny room with one vast architectural object, such as an ancient iron gate, a marble column or a distressed plaster bust in an alcove will look dramatic. Treat such a vintage find as art: set it against a blank wall, light it beautifully and allow its full glory to shine. Like all your other carefully chosen vintage treasures, this one has a story to tell.

LEFT If you have large-scale vintage items to show off, consider ways to highlight them. Here, midnight blue walls and violet upholstery create a moody background – the perfect foil for the exotic-looking lamp and the gilded rococo mirror.

OPPOSITE Treat an unusual architectural salvage buy as art. In this very classical room, a vintage metal radiator, rusty and raw, looks like an amazing piece of sculpture. Note the angled lamp, which can spotlight the piece by night.

Displaying china and glass

- Clean vintage china before you display it: wash porcelain in warm soapy water, but if the glaze is cracked, just wipe gently with a damp cloth.

- Add white vinegar to the rinsing water when cleaning vintage glass, to avoid fogging. A rolled-up piece of newspaper left inside soaks up remaining moisture.

- Dust your collections using a soft sable brush, rather than with a cloth that may snag on rough areas.

There are two things to consider when displaying precious china and glass: making an eye-catching display but keeping it out of harm's reach, so choose somewhere far from vibrations and direct heat. Show off china on a mantelpiece, a console table or on open shelves, or wall-mount plates using plate holders. A glass collection looks dramatic arranged so natural light can shine through – close to a window or on glass shelves – or in front of a mirror to create pretty reflections. Glass vases arranged in descending order look dramatic. Turn pottery figures into a sociable inward-looking circle rather than arranging them in a line. Mix up china and glass using colour, period style or shape as the theme. And ring the changes regularly so displays don't become stale.

OPPOSITE AND ABOVE Arranging objects by colour – turquoise for glass, curtains and a butterfly, or clear glass against a white wall – is very effective.

RIGHT A sense of fun can make a display. This collection of tin figures, gazing expectantly at an eccentric vintage Bambi lamp, draws the eye.

Suppliers

AUSTRALIA

CIRCA-C20
78a Campbell Street
Surry Hills, NSW
Tel: + 61 (0) 2 9212 2557
circa-c20.com.au
Specialists in 20th-century
glass and ceramics.

GREAT DANE
613 Elizabeth Street
Redfern
NSW 2016
Tel: + 61 (0) 2 9699 7677
greatdanefurniture.com
Specialists in mid-20th century
Scandinavian furniture,
lighting, textiles and
accessories.

VINTAGE ATTIC
PO Box 142
Hazelbrook
NSW 2779
Tel: + 61 (0) 2 4758 6919
vintageattic.com.au
Vintage eiderdowns, linens and
lace from the Victorian era to
the 70s.

USA

HANNAHS TREASURES
PO Box 326
Harlan
Iowa 51537
Tel: + 1 866 755 3173
hannahstreasures.com
Vast collection of vintage
wallpapers from the 20s to the
60s in over 500 designs.

HISTORIC HOUSEPARTS
540 South Avenue
Rochester
NY 14620
Tel: + 1 585 325 2329
historichouseparts.com
Wonderful resource for antique
door furniture, radiators,
sanitaryware, fireplaces and
more.

HOUSE VERNACULAR
59 Ontario Street
Honeoye Falls
NY 14472

Tel: + 1 585 469 0908
housevernacular.com
Specialists in affordable,
authentic wallpaper designs
reproduced from historic
sources, from Victorian to Art
Nouveau and beyond, plus a
custom service.

MELINA MADE
1235 Watson Ranch Way
Dixon
CA 95620
Tel: + 1 707 365 5618
melinamade.com
Fabulous vintage inspired
patterns on barkcloth fabrics,
wallpapers, glassware and
accessories from the mid-20th
century.

MODERN LIVING
Tel: + 1 610 304 6588
modernlivingusa.com
Established in 1977, specialists
in 20th-century design
furniture, lighting and
accessories.

REPRO DEPOT
Tel: + 1 413 527 4047
reprodepot.com
Wonderful selection of
reproduction vintage cotton
fabrics, ribbons and trims, some
based on authentic designs.

ROSIE'S VINTAGE WALLPAPER
Tel: + 1 618 732 6275
rosiesvintagewallpaper.com
Inspiring website with vast
selection of vintage papers in
many categories, from foil to
flock, children's wallpapers to
papers of the 70s.

SECONDHAND ROSE
138 Duane Street
New York
NY 10013
Tel: + 1 212 393 9002
secondhandrose.com
Lovely store in New York with
huge selection of original
wallpapers dating as far back
as Art Nouveau, plus original
linoleum, lamps and fixtures.

VINTAGE TUB & BATH
534 West Green Street
Hazleton
PA 18201
Tel: + 1 877 868 1369
vintagetub.com
Fantastic selection of copper
and cast-iron bath styles,
including slipper, roll top and
pedestal styles, plus
reproduction period-style taps.

EUROPE

ARCHITECTURAL CLASSICS
Princess Court
Gloucester Street South
Dublin 2
Ireland
Tel: + 353 (1) 677 3557
architecturalclassics.com
Showroom and online shop
with wonderful original door
furniture from the 19th century
to the 1920s, plus an excellent
reproduction section.

DECAYING ELEGANCE
Rue du Val du Moulin
Hauteville sur Mer Manche
Normandie 50590
France
Tel: + 33 (2) 33 07 66 97
decaying-elegance.co.uk
Beautiful, ever-changing
selection of vintage and
antique furniture, mirrors,
garden pieces, lighting and
architectural items.

5QM
Herczeg & Sassmannshausen
GbR
Gladbacher Str. 35
50672 Köln
Germany
Tel: +49 221 2948455
5qm.de
Very large selection of vintage
wallpapers from the 50s, 60s
and 70s.

GLAS-DESIGN
glas-design.nl
Specialists in mid 20th-century
Scandinavian glass, but also
ceramics, lighting and design.

INTERIOR 1900
Magnus Karisson
Skogsv.8
532 32 Gotene
Sweden
Tel: +46 (0) 511 341 100
interior1900.com
Fabulous selection of vintage
wallpapers from 1890 to 1980s,
plus original 50s door handles,
hooks and lighting.

LILY AND AGATHE
12 Bis Rue Denis Diderot
66000 Perpignan
France
Tel: +33 (0) 8 70 46 67 97
lilyandagathe.com
Original vintage children's
games, home accessories
made from vintage fabrics, and
novelty gifts.

SWIET
Leuken 117
3920 Lommel
Belgium
Tel: +32 (0) 11 51 51 41
swiet-vintage.com
Fantastically eclectic selection
of vintage furniture, wallpaper,
casual crockery, beds and more.

VINTAGE WALLPAPERS
Poortakkerstraat 1
9051 St Denijs Westrem
Belgium
Tel: +32 (0) 477 980 355
vintagewallpapers.be
Original vintage wallpapers
and vinyl wallcoverings from
the 60s and 70s in many
colours.

UK

Architectural Salvage
LASSCO
30 Wandsworth Road
London SW8 2LG
Tel: +44 (0) 20 7394 2100
lassco.co.uk
A vast selection of salvaged
pieces and architectural
antiques, everything from
quirky furniture to radiators,
bathroom fittings and
hardware.

RETROUVIUS
2A Ravensworth Road
Kensal Green
London NW10 5NR
Tel: +44 (0) 20 8960 6060
retrouvius.co.uk
Architectural salvage and
design, with an innovative mix
of reclaimed furniture,
surfaces and architectural
antiques.

TRAINSPOTTERS
Unit 1, The Warehouse
Libby Drive
Stroud
Gloucestershire GL5 1RN
Tel: +44 (0) 1453 756677
trainspotters.uk.com
Dealers in selected
architectural salvaged and
period decorative items, with
an emphasis on 20th-century
and industrial fittings and
fixtures.

WINCHCOMBE RECLAMATION
Broadway Road
Winchcombe
Cheltenham
Gloucestershire GL54 5NT
Tel: +44 (0) 1242 609564
winchcombereclamation.co.uk
Reclaimed fireplaces, sinks,
mirrors and radiators, plus
salvaged building materials.

20th Century Style Information Sites
RETRO WOW
retrowow.co.uk
Online information resource
for the 50s, 60s and 70s, with
information on furniture, TV,
lighting, style and entertaining.

Vintage Furniture and Accessories
BAILEYS HOME AND GARDEN
Whitecross Farm
Bridstow
Herefordshire HR9 6JU
Tel: +44 (0) 1989 561931
baileyshomeandgarden.com
Beautiful reproduction taps,
butler's sinks and lighting, plus
salvaged items from industrial
lamps to shoe lasts.

BROWNRIGG @ HOME
1 Pound Street
Petworth
West Sussex GU28 0DX
Tel: +44 (0) 1798 344321
brownrigg-interiors.com
Excellent selection of antique
furniture, with a very good
stock of leather armchairs.

FADE INTERIORS,
17 Oxford Street
Woodstock
Oxford OX20 1TH
Tel: +44 (0) 1993 811655
fadeinteriors.com
Shop and website with
decorative vintage furniture
and accessories from 50s
eiderdowns to knitted tea
cosies and old French linens.

FRENCH FINDS
Strangman Street
Leek
Staffordshire ST13 5DU
Tel: +44 (0) 1538 370052
frenchfinds.co.uk
From 19th-century armoires to
antique beds and mirrors.

THE ODD CHAIR COMPANY
The Plaza
535 Kings Road
London SW10 0SZ
Tel: +44 (0) 20 7352 4700
theoddchaircompany.com
Large stock of traditionally
restored antique upholstered
furniture; they also offer a
finder service for any design.

VINTAGE HOME
Pottery Cottage
Horsecroft Lane
Stanford-in-the-Vale
Nr Faringdon
Oxfordshire SN7 8LL
Tel: +44 (0) 1367 718993
vintage-home.co.uk
Shabby chic style vintage
homewares, from textiles to
bedding, china to pictures.

20th Century Vintage Specialists
CHA CHA CHA
20/22 Avenue Mews
London N10 3NP
Tel: +44 (0) 20 773 951 7855
cha-cha-cha.co.uk
Mid 20th-century furniture,

lighting and fabrics, plus new
lampshades made from old
fabrics.

DECORATUM
13- 25 Church Street
London NW8 8DT
Tel: +44 (0) 20 7724 6969
decoratum.com
Vast stock of vintage furniture,
mainly 50s and 60s, including
furniture, art and original
textiles.

FEARS AND KAHN
Unit 7B, Criftin Enterprise
Centre
Oxton Road
Epperstone
Nottinghamshire NG14 6AT
Tel: +44 (0) 1623 882170
fearsandkahn.co.uk
Mid 20th-century furniture,
lighting, rugs and vintage
posters.

FRAGILE DESIGN
14/15 The Custard Factory
Digbeth
Birmingham B9 4AA
Tel: +44 (0) 121 224 7378
fragiledesign.com
Specialists in 20th-century
vintage design including
furniture, ceramics, glassware,
art and textiles.

GUNPOWDER HOUSE
Tel: +44 (0) 8224 3550
gunpowderhouse.com
Ever-changing selection of
vintage telephones, lighting,
clocks and bathroom cabinets,
some restored.

HOME SWEET HOMESTYLE
5 Haystoun Park
Willingdon
Eastbourne BN22 0NN
Tel: +44 (0) 1323 504345
homesweethomestyle.co.uk
Eclectic selection of vintage
homewares, mainly from the
40s and 50s.

I WANT VINTAGE
PO Box 8773
Coalville LE67 0BN
Tel: +44 (0) 845 053 3474
iwantvintage.co.uk
Website offering a "virtual
vintage town", bringing

together lots of vintage
dealers in many categories,
from soft furnishings to
furniture.

THE MODERN WAREHOUSE
243B Victoria Park Road
London E9 7HD
Tel: +44 (0) 20 8986 0740
themodernwarehouse.com
Specialists in mid-century
modern furniture; also a
consultancy service.

RE-FOUND OBJECTS, RE
Bishops Yard
Main Street
Corbridge
Northumberland NE45 5LA
Tel: +44 (0) 1434 634567
re-foundobjects.com
Store and website offering
reclaimed and salvaged
furniture and accessories, plus
reproduction vintage lighting,
hardware, garden accessories
and textiles.

RETRO ART
Tel: +44 (0) 115 847 5945
retroart.co.uk
Specialists in Scandinavian,
American and British art and
furniture from 1880 to 1980.

RETRODECADES
retrodecades.com
Wonderful selection of mid-
20th century furniture and
accessories, including an
excellent selection of period
phones.

20th CENTURY MARKS
Tel: +44 (0) 1474 872460
20thcenturymarks.co.uk
Dealers in 20th-century vintage
furniture, including great
lighting, textiles and a
wonderful selection of
electrical goods, including
funky 70s TVs.

Beds
AFTER NOAH
261 Kings Road
London SW3 5EL
Tel: +44 (0) 20 7351 2610
afternoah.com
Excellent selection of restored
and unrestored double and
single beds - mainly cast-iron

bedsteads – plus vintage-style telephones, lighting and accessories.

LA MAISON
107– 108 Shoreditch High Street
London E1 6JN
Tel: +44 (0) 20 7729 9646
atlamaison.com
Vast selection of antique French beds, from single to double and daybeds, plus workshop and mattresses made to size.

SWANS OF OAKHAM
17 Mill Street
Oakham
Rutland LE15 6EA
Tel: +44 (0) 1572 724364
antiquefrenchbeds.co.uk
Lovely selection of late 19th-century and early 20th-century, mainly French, beds, plus handmade mattresses made to order.

Vintage Bedlinens
ANTIQUE VINTAGE DESIGNS
antique-vintage-designs.co.uk
Wonderful accessories including aprons, cushions and bags, made to order using antique and vintage textiles including French antique linens.

ENGLISH EIDERDOWN
Keys Mail Order Warehouse
Stephenson Road
Clacton on Sea
Essex CO15 4XA
Tel: +44 (0) 1255 432518
englisheiderdown.co.uk
Duck-down eiderdowns made to order in traditional designs, including Art Deco motifs.

Bathrooms
THE BATH WORKS
Glenacres
Watling Street
Kensworth
Bedfordshire LU6 3QS
Tel: +44 (0) 1582 602713
thebathworks.com
Beautiful selection of restored antique baths, including slipper, double and bateau styles and many types of finishes including copper.

CATCHPOLE & RYE
Saracens Dairy
Jobbs Lane
Pluckley
Kent TN27 0SA
Tel: +44 (0) 1233 840840
crye.co.uk
Specialists in beautiful copies of vintage sanitaryware, plus original baths, basins and baths in many styles.

DRUMMONDS
78 Royal Hospital Road
London SW3 4HN
Tel: +44 (0) 20 7376 4499
drummonds-arch.co.uk
Architectural antiques specialist offering restored baths; also beautiful range of cast-iron baths with traditional enamelling based on old designs.

THE WATER MONOPOLY
16/18 Lonsdale Road
London NW6 6RD
Tel: +44 (0) 20 7624 2636
watermonopoly.com
Beautiful baths, basins, WCs and showers in period styles but also a selection of restored antique pieces.

Kitchens
SOURCE ANTIQUES
Victoria Park Business Centre
Bath BA1 3AX
Tel: +44 (0) 1225 469200
source-antiques.co.uk
Specialists in restored 50s kitchens and appliances, especially the English Rose and Boulton & Paul brands.

JOHN LEWIS OF HUNGERFORD
156– 158 Wandsworth Bridge Road
London SW6 2UH
Tel: +44 (0) 20 7371 5603
john-lewis.co.uk
Authentic-looking copies of 50s kitchens in four bright colours.

SMEG
Tel: +44 (0) 870 990 9907
smeguk.com
Modern retro-styled fridges and dishwashers.

20th Century Glass and Ceramics
ARTEFACT ONLINE
artefactonline.com
Informative and useful website specialising in ceramics from the early 20th century to the present day, but with a particular interest in the 50s and 60s.

CHANCE GLASS
chanceglass.net
Information site for collectors of Chance Glass, including the popular handkerchief designs.

CHINASEARCH
4 Princes Drive
Kenilworth
Warwickshire CV8 2FD
Tel: +44 (0) 1926 512402
chinasearch.co.uk
Suppliers of discontinued china and tableware, plus glassware and cutlery.

GLASS ROOTS
glass-roots.co.uk
Specialists in stylish mid 20th-century glass and collectibles.

MUM HAD THAT
mumhadthat.com
Scandinavian and British mid 20th-century glass, ceramics and metal, plus oddities such as typewriters and old TVs.

PIPS TRIP
13 Pyne Road
Surbiton
Surrey KT6 7BN
Tel: +44 (0) 8451 650274
pips-trip.co.uk
Specialists in retro/vintage china and glass from the 50s, 60s and 70s.

WHITEFRIARS
whitefriars.com
The official website for collectors of Whitefriars glass.

Mirrors
OLD FRENCH MIRRORS
Tel: +44 (0) 1189 482444
oldfrenchmirrors.com
Specialists in 19th-century French antique mirrors of many types.

ON REFLECTION
Bullen Farmhouse
Horse Lane
Charlton Horethorne
Sherborne
Dorset DT9 4NL
Tel: +44 (0) 1963 220723
on-reflection.co.uk
Family-run business with over 150 antique mirrors in stock, sympathetically restored.

Lighting
THE ANTIQUE CHANDELIER
47 West Street
Dorking
Surrey RH4 1BU
Tel: +44 (0) 1306 882004
theantiquechandelier.co.uk
Specialists in antique chandeliers of many types and styles.

GEOFFREY HARRIS LIGHTING
537 Battersea Park Road
London SW11 3BL
Tel: +44 (0) 20 7228 6101
geoffreyharris.co.uk
Lighting retailer with excellent selection of classic design lighting, from the Louis Poulsen range from Denmark to the Bestlite range from the 30s.

MATHMOS
Tel: +44 (0) 1202 644 600
mathmos.com
Various versions of the original lava lamp, plus funky space projector lights for a 70s mood.

PERIOD STYLE LIGHTING
The Barn
Foxholes Farm
London Road
Hertford Heath
Hertfordshire SG13 7NT
Tel: +44 (0) 1992 554943
periodstylelighting.co.uk
A good mix of antique lighting, plus period reproductions including Art Deco styles, and a lighting workshop.

STELLA CHRISTIE LIGHTING
Tel: +44 (0) 7967 603548
stellachristielighting.co.uk
Specialists in floor, table and side lamps by key 20th-century designers such as Eileen Gray and Christian Dell.

Hardware

HOLLOWAYS OF LUDLOW
121 Shepherd's Bush Road
Hammersmith
London W6 7LP
Tel: +44 (0) 20 7602 5757
hollowaysofludlow.com
Wonderful reproductions of
cast-iron radiators, lighting,
door knobs and hardware.

JG TOOLS
Units 19/20
27a Wallace Crescent
Carshalton
Surrey SM5 3SU
Tel: +44 (0) 20 8669 4570
cast-iron-radiators-
restoration.co.uk
Vast stock of original cast-iron
radiators, all restored, safety
tested and guaranteed.

THE CAST IRON
RECLAMATION COMPANY
The Courtyard
Preston Court Farm
Bookham
Surrey
Tel: +44 (0) 20 8977 5977
perfect-irony.com
Wonderful selection of both
restored and reproduction
radiators in many styles, plus
original radiator covers, baths,
and fireplaces.

Vintage Textiles

BEYOND FRANCE
Tel: +44 (0) 1285 641867
beyondfrance.co.uk
Hand-loomed vintage linens,
grain sacks and Hungarian cart
covers, plus vintage
haberdashery.

CHARLOTTE CASADEJUS
Tel: +44 (0) 7378 9755
charlottecasadejus.com
Beautiful cushions and
accessories made using 19th-
century antique
monogrammed linens.

COUNTRY HOUSE ANTIQUE
TEXTILES
Lendon House
Abbotsham
Bideford
Devon EX39 5BW
Tel: +44 (0) 1237 42069
countryhouseantiquetextiles.co.uk

Vast selection of vintage
textiles from the 19th century
to the 70s, including a
childrens' selection and
contemporary vintage-inspired
fabrics.

REVAMPIT
52 Grafton Road
London W3 6PD
Tel: +44 (0) 20 8354 7354
revampit.co.uk
Cushions, pegbags, bunting
and home accessories made
from recycled and vintage
cotton, denim and linen.

Paints

FARROW & BALL
249 Fulham Road
London SW3 6HY
Tel: +44 (0) 20 7351 0273
farrow-ball.com
Wide range of period paint
colours, plus traditionally made
wallpapers made using
authentic period designs.

THE LITTLE GREENE PAINT
COMPANY
Wood Street
Openshaw
Manchester M11 2FB
Tel: +44 (0) 161 230 0880
thelittlegreene.com
Wonderful range of heritage
paint colours, plus period-
design wallpapers.

Vintage and Vintage Style
Wallpapers

THE ART OF WALLPAPER
Unit 3, Robert Harvey Wall
Long Stratton
Norfolk NR15 2FD
Tel: +44 (0) 1508 531171
theartofwallpaper.co.uk
High-quality wallpaper printer,
with nostalgic and retro-style
wallpapers.

CONCEPT COVERINGS
The Design Studio
Regents Park
2 Wisteria Drive
Lower Darwen
Lancashire BB3 0QY
Tel: +44 (0) 1254 680266
conceptcoverings.co.uk
Digital wallpaper printers, who
can create a customised
wallpaper from a vintage scrap.

E W MOORE & SON
39-43 Plashet Grove
London E6 1AD
Tel: +44 (0) 20 8471 9392
ewmoore.co.uk
Family wallpaper firm
established in 1906, with a
great range of ever-changing
vintage wallpapers from the
60s to the 80s.

GRAHAM & BROWN
Tel:+ 44 0800 328 8452
grahamandbrown.co.uk
Plenty of funky 60s- and 70s-
inspired wallpapers, plus a
groovy range designed by
Barbara Hulanicki.

Carpets and Rugs

BRONTE CARPETS
Bankfield Mill
Greenfield Road
Colne
Lancs BB8 9PD
Tel: +44 (0) 1282 862736
brontecarpets.co.uk
100% pure new wool shag-pile
carpets in 40 stock colours.

CLASSIC MODERN
classic-modern.co.uk
20th-century specialists, with a
good selection of vintage rugs
from the 50s, 60s and 70s.

THE RUG COMPANY
124 Holland Park Avenue
London W11 4UE
Tel: +44 (0) 20 7229 5148
therugcompany.info
New rugs of many types,
including classic needlepoint,
Aubusson and pop-art style
funky designs.

Natural Fibre Flooring

THE ALTERNATIVE FLOORING
COMPANY
3B Stephensons Close
East Portway
Andover
Hampshire SP10 3RU
Tel: +44 (0) 1264 335111
alternativeflooring.com
Excellent selection of many
natural fibre floorings, from
coir and sisal to wool mixes.

CRUCIAL TRADING
The Plaza
535 Kings Road
London SW10 0SZ
Tel: +44 (0) 20 7376 7100
crucial-trading.com
Wide range of coir, jute, sisal
and seagrass, and wool.

Stone Flooring

FIRED EARTH
3 Twyford Mill
Oxford Road
Adderbury
Nr Banbury
Oxfordshire OX17 3SX
Tel: +44 (0) 1295 812088
firedearth.com
Very wide range of new stone
flooring in a choice of
terracotta, slate and stone,
some with antiqued effects.

STONELL
521- 525 Battersea Park Road
London SW11 3BN
Tel: + 44 0800 083 2282
stonell.com
Good selection of hand-aged
stone tiles, tumbled stone,
honed limestone and riven
slate.

Wood Flooring

THE ANTIQUE OAK FLOORING
COMPANY
94 High Street
London N8 7NT
Tel: +44 (0) 20 8347 8222
antiqueoakflooring.com
Range of oak and pine
reclaimed floorboards, in wide
and narrow plank sizes.

VICTORIAN WOODWORKS
54 River Road
Creekmouth
Barking
Essex IG11 0DW
Tel: +44 (0) 20 8534 1000
victorianwoodworks.co.uk
Specialists in reclaimed wood
flooring, sourced from all over
the world.

Architects & Designers

1100 Architects
435 Hudson Street
8th Floor
New York
New York 10014
Tel: + 1 (212) 645 1011

A La Carter
109 Mile End Road
London E1 4UJ
Tel: +44 (0) 20 7790 0259

Atelier d'Architecture M
Frisenna SCPL
15 rue de Verviers
4020 Liège
Belgium
Tel: + 32 (0) 4 341 5786

Azman Architects
18 Charlotte Road
Shoreditch
London EC2A 3PB
Tel: + 44 (0) 20 7739 8191

Bruce Bierman Design Inc.
29th West 15th Street
New York
New York 10011
USA
Tel: +1 (212) 243 1935

Buttazzoni, Laurent
62 rue de Montreuil
75011 Paris
France
Tel: + 33 (0)1 40 09 98 49

Caproni Associates Inc
200 Central Park South
New York
New York 10019
USA
Tel: +1 (212) 977 4010

Cherner, Ben
Tel: +1 (212) 475 5656

Collin, Fred
Bransdale Lodge
Bransdale Fadmor
York YO62 7JL
Tel: + 44 (0) 1751 431 137

Coorengel & Calvagrac
43 rue de l'Echiquier
75010 Paris
France

Tel: + 33 (0) 1 40 27 14 65

Curtis Wood Architects
The Shopfront
84 Haberdashers Street
London N1 6EJ
Tel: + 44 (0) 20 7684 1400

Delsalle, J F
3 rue Seguier
75006 Paris
France
Tel: + 33 (0) 1 43 29 42 76

Diamond Baratta Design Inc
270 Lafayette Street
New York
New York 10012
USA
Tel: +1 (212) 966 8892

Dominique Picquier
Tel: + 33 (0)1 42 72 39 14
Emery & Cie
12 rue de Lausanne
10060 Brussels
Belgium
Tel: + 32 (0) 2 513 5892

F T Architecture & Interiors
Peter Franck & Kathleen Triem
59 Letter S Road
Ghent
New York 12075
USA
Tel: +1 (518) 392 3721

Faulkner, Frank
92 North 5th Street
Hudson
New York 12534
USA
Tel: +1 (518) 828 2295

Fougeron Architecture
720 York Street
Suite 107
San Francisco
California 94110
Tel: +1 (415) 641 5744

Fox Linton Associates
Tel: + 44 (0) 20 7622 0920

Galerie Yves Gastou
12 rue Bonaparte
75006 Paris
France

Tel: + 33 (0) 1 53 73 00 10

Gene Leedy
555 Avenue G NW
Winter Haven
Florida 33880
USA
Tel: + 1 (863) 293 7173

Guy Peterson FAIA
1234 First Street
Sarasota
Florida 34236
USA
Tel: + 1 (941) 952 1111

Hambro, Nathalie
63 Warwick Square
London SW1V 2AL
Tel: + 44 (0) 20 7834 1122

IPL Interiors
Studio 4a
75-81 Burnaby Street
London SW10 0NS
Tel: + 44 (0) 20 7978 4224

James Mohn Design
245 West 29th Street
Suite 504
New York
New York 10001
USA
Tel: + 1 (212) 414 1477

John Barman Inc
500 Park Avenue
Suite 21a
New York
New York 10022
USA
Tel: + 1 (212) 838 9443

Koskinen, Ulla
Untamonte 4a
00610 Helsinki
Finland
Tel: + 35 8 0868 35450

La Rizza, Baldassare
London House
Suite 13a
266 Fulham Road
London SW10 9EL
Tel: + 44 (0) 20 7351 5771

Lété, Nathalie
Tel: + 33 (0) 1 49 60 84 76

Lincoln, Angi
Tel: + 44 (0) 7957 621796

Marc Prosman Architecten Bv
Overtoom 197
1054 HT Amsterdam
The Netherlands
Tel: + 31 (0) 204 892 099

Matlock Architects, Audrey
88 West Broadway
New York
New York 10007
USA
Tel: + 1 (212) 267 2378

Méchiche, Frédéric
14 rue Saint Croix de la
Bretonne
75004 Paris
France
Tel: + 33 (0) 1 42 78 78 28

Michael Wolfson Architects
(London, England)
Tel: + 44 (0) 20 7630 9377

Next Architects
Weesperzijde 93
1091 EK Amsterdam
The Netherlands
Tel: + 31 (0) 20 463 0463

Ogawa Depardon Architects
137 Varick Street # 404
New York
New York 10013
USA
Tel: + 1 (212) 627 7390

Pamplemousse Design Inc
Delphine Krakoff
Tel: + 1 (212) 980 2033

Pierre D'Avoine Architects
54-58 Tanner Street
London SE1 3PH
Tel: + 44 (0) 20 7403 7220

Proudlock, Lena
4 The Chipping
Tetbury
Gloucestershire GL8 8ET
Tel: + 44 (0)1666 503934

Rashid, Karim
357 West 17th Street
New York

New York 10011
USA
Tel: + 1 (212) 929 8657

Renoird, Emmanuel
18 rue de Bourgogne
75007 Paris
France
Tel: + 33 (0) 1 45 56 99 24

Resistance Design
Eric Mailaender
11 Tompkins Place, No.2
Brooklyn
New York 11231
USA
Tel: + 1 (212) 714 0448

Selldorf Architects
62 White Street
New York
New York 10013
USA
Tel: + 1 (212) 219 9571

Sera of London
3 Lonsdale Road
Notting Hill Gate
London W11 2BY
Tel: + 44 (0) 20 7286 5948

Shelton, Mindel & Associates
143 West 20th Street
New York
New York 10011
USA
Tel: + 1 (212) 243 3939

Sheppard Day Limited
The Friary
47 Francis Road
Lodnon SW1P 1QR
Tel: + 44 (0) 20 7821 2222

Sills Huniford Associates
30 East 67th Street
New York
New York 10021
USA
Tel: + 1 (212) 243 3939

Solis Betancourt
1739 Connecticut Avenue NW
Washington
DC 20009
USA
Tel: + 1 (202) 659 8734

Studio Sofield Inc.
Emma O'Neill
Tel: + 1 (232) 473 1300

Terry Hunziker Inc
208 Third Avenue Street
Seattle
Washington 98104
USA
Tel: + 1 (206) 467 1144

Van de Walle, Alex
Vlaamsesteenweg 3
1000 Brussels
Belgium
Tel: + 32 (0) 477 806 676

Vicente Wolf Associates Inc
333 West 39th Street
10th Floor
New York
New York 10018
USA
Tel: + 1 (212) 465 0590

Vignot, Nicolas
6 rue Vaucouleurs
75011 Paris
France
Tel: + 33 (0) 6 11 96 67 69

Artists & Makers

Hunt Slonem's Studio
545 West 45th Street 4th Floor
New York
New York 10036
Tel: + 1 (212) 620 4835

Rupert Spira
Ceramicist, UK
Tel: + 44 (0)1588 650588

Manufacturers & Suppliers

Casa Lopez
27 Boulevard Raspail
75007 Paris
France
Tel: + 33 (0)1 45 48 30 97

Century Design
68 Marylebone High Street
London W1U 5JH
Tel: + 44 (0) 20 7487 5100

Cola Red
Classic Retro Furniture
Woodbury House
1a Grosvenor Road
Northwood
Middx HA6 3HH
Tel: + 44 (0) 1923 820300

CVO Firevault
36 Great Titchfield Street
London W1W 8BQ
Tel: + 44 (0) 207 580 5333

Hubert Zandberg Interiors
Goldborne Road
London W10 5PS
Tel: + 44 (0) 20 8962 2776

Jospehine Ryan Antiques
63 Abbeville Road
London SW4 9JW
Tel: + 44 (0) 20 8675 3900

Thomas Kjaerholm
Rungstedvej 86
2960 Rungsted Kyst
Demark
Tel: + 45 (0) 45 76 56 56

Traditions by Pamela Kline
P O Box 416
Claverack
New York 12513
Tel: + 1 (518) 851 3975

Wallpaper

Graham & Brown Wallpaper
P O Box 39
India Mill
Harwood Street
Blackburn
Lancashire BB1 3DB
Tel: + 44 (0) 1254 691 321

Marian Cotterill Wallpapers
Lounge (London) Limited
6 Mapesbury Road
London NW2 4HY
Tel: + 44 (0) 20 8931 6649

Historic Properties

Historic New England
Harrison Gray Otis House
141 Cambridge Street
Boston
MA 02114
Tel: + 1 (617) 227 3956

Fabric designers

Indigo Seas
Lynn von Kersting
123 North Robertson
Boulevard
Los Angeles
California 90048
Tel: + 1 (310) 550 8758

Jane Churchill
Tel: + 44 (0) 20 8874 6484

Les Editions Dominique
Kieffer
8 rue Herold
75001 Paris
France
Tel: + 33 (0) 1 42 21 32 44

Linum France sas
ZAC du Tourail
Coustellet
84660 Maubec
France
Tel: + 33 (0) 4 90 76 34 00

Picture Acknowledgements

PHOTOGRAPHERS' CREDITS

Ken Hayden 41 above left, 57, 67, 68-69, 76, 84, 114 above & 127 left

Lucinda Symons front cover, 11 above left, 28 left, 56, 58 & 73

Chris Tubbs 22

Simon Upton 1-7, 11 above right, centre & below, 12-13, 14, 16-25, 26 above, 27, 30-31, 34-37, 41 above right & centre, 42, 46, 47 below left, 49, 51, 52-55, 59, 60 left, 61 left, 63, 66 below, 72, 77, 80, 81 left, 82, 85, 86,88 right & left, 89, 90-91, 93 above, centre left & below, 94, 97 above left & below, 100 right, 102 above and below left, 103, 104, 106, 107 below, 108, 109 left, 116, 127 right, 128-131, 133 & 135

Frédéric Vasseur 15, 32-33, 60 right, 61 right, 66 above, 76, 83, 95, 96 right, 97 above right, 111, 114 below right, 115, 120 below, 122-123 & 126

Fritz von der Schulenburg 29 & 79

Luke White 132 & 134

Andrew Wood 8-9, 23, 26 below, 38-39, 41 below, 43-45, 47 above & below right, 50, 62, 64-65, 74-75, 78, 81 right, 87, 93 centre right, 96 left, 98-99, 100 left, 101, 102 below right, 105, 107 above, 109 right, 110, 112-113, 114 below left, 117-119, 120 above, 121 & 123-125

LOCATION CREDITS
1 Mark Gilbey & Polly Dickens' house in Pennsylvania; 2 Frank Faulkner's house in Upstate New York; 3 Rupert & Caroline Spira's house in Shropshire; 3 below centre Michael Coorengel & Jean-Pierre Calvagac's apartment in Paris; 3 below right designed by Frédéric Méchiche; 4 Yvonne Sporre's house in London, designed by J F Delsalle; 5 the home of Peri Wolfman and Charles Gold in Bridgehampton; 7 designed by Frédéric Méchiche; 8-9 a house in East Hampton, designed by Selldorf Architects; 11 above left Lounge (London) Ltd/Marian Cotterill Wallpapers; 11 above right Emmanuel Renoird's house in Normandy; 11 centre left a house in France, decorated by Yves Gastou; 11 centre right Véronique Lopez's house from Casa Lopez; 11 below left Hubert Zandberg's apartment in London; 11 below right designed by Frédéric Méchiche; 14 Pamela Kline (of Traditions)'s home in Claverack, New York; 15 Eric Mailaender's apartment in New York, designed by Resistance Design; 16 a home featuring Jane Churchill fabrics; 17 Hubert Zandberg's apartment in London; 18 Hanne Kjaerholm's house in Copenhagen, Denmark; 19 left Diane de Clercq's home in Rome; 19 right Reed Krakoff's apartment in New York, designed in collaboration with Pamplemousse Design; 20 designed by Frédéric Méchiche; 21 Rupert & Caroline Spira's house in Shropshire; 23 Neilama Residence, designed by Ulla Koskinen; 24 John Barman's apartment in New York; 26 above Rupert & Caroline Spira's house in Shropshire; 26 below Anna Bonde's house in Provence; 27 Chris Bortugno's house in Upstate New York; 28 left Lounge (London) Ltd/Marian Cotterill Wallpapers; 28 right Denise Seegals' apartment in New York, designed by Sonja & John Caproni; 29 Sera Hersham Loftus' house in London; 30 Emmanuel Renoird's house in Normandy; 31 above designed by Frédéric Méchiche; 31 below Walter Gropius House, a property of Historic New England (HistoricNewEngland.org); 32-33 Dominique Picquier's house in Paris; 34 Charles de Selliers' house in Brussels; 35 Agnès Emery's house in Brussels; 36 Frank Faulkner's Catskill home; 37 John Barman's apartment in New York; 38-39 Stark residence, London, designed by Curtis Wood; 41 above left designed by Jackie Villevoye; 41 above right a house in France, decorated by Yves Gastou; 41 centre left Rupert & Caroline Spira's house in Shropshire; 41 centre right Josephine Ryan's house in London; 41 below left Agathe Gérin's apartment in New Delhi; 41 below right Katy Barker's Paris apartment, designed by Laurent Buttazzoni; 42 Yvonne Sporre's house in London, designed by J F Delsalle; 43 Karim Rashid's apartment in New York; 44 Dominique Kieffer's apartment in Paris; 45 Angela Carr's house in London, designed by Azman Owens; 46 Josephine Ryan's house in London; 47 above left Weaving/Thomasson residence, Essex; 47 above right Fred & Helen Collin's house in London; 47 below left Hanne Kjaerholm's house in Copenhagen, Denmark; 47 below right Anne Fourgeron's house in San Francisco; 48 Cola Red; 49 Glen Senk and Keith Johnson's house in Philadelphia; 50 Tony Baratta's house in Long Island; 51 Chris Bortugno's house in Upstate New York; 52-53 Walter Gropius House, a property of Historic New England (HistoricNewEngland.org); 54 Dominique Lubar's apartment in London; 55 Anthony Cochran's apartment in New York; 56 Lounge (London) Ltd/Marian Cotterill Wallpapers; 57 Maureen Paley's house in London; 58 Graham & Brown Wallpapers; 59 above David Carter's house in London; 59 below Yvonne Sporre's house in London, designed by J F Delsalle; 60 left Peter Franck & Kathleen Triem's house in Ghent, New York; 60 right Nicolas Vignot's apartment in Paris; 61 left Frank Faulkner's Catskill home; 61 right Ben Cherner & Emma O'Neill's apartment in New York, designed by Emma O'Neill; 62 Fishman residence, Florida, interiors by Wilson Stiles, Sarasota, Florida, architect Guy Peterson FAIA; 63 John Barman's apartment in New York; 64-65 Weaving/Thomasson residence, Essex; 66 above Nathalie Lété's house in Paris; 66 below a loft apartment designed by Ushida Findlay; 67 designers Keith Day and Peter Sheppard; 68-69 designed by Terry Hunziker; 70-71 Graham & Brown Wallpapers; 72 left Emmanuel Renoird's house in Normandy; 73 Lounge (London) Limited/Marianne Cotterill Wallpapers; 74 Anna Bonde's house in Provençe; 74-75 Bob & Pam Levin's house in Bel Air, designed by Lynn von Kersting; 75 Weaving/Thomasson residence, London;

76 Lena Proudlock's house in Gloucestershire; 77 Walter Gropius House, a property of Historic New England (HistoricNewEngland.org); 78 left Springman Westover residence, London; 78 right Neilama Residence, designed by Ulla Koskinen; 79 designed by Agnès Comar; 80 Reed Krakoff's apartment in New York, designed in collaboration with Pamplemousse Design; 81 left Walter Gropius House, a property of Historic New England (HistoricNewEngland.org); 81 right Shane/Cooper residence, New York designed by 1100 Architects; 82 left Wingate Jackson, Jr and Paul Trantanella's house in Upstate New York; 82 right Walter Gropius House, a property of Historic New England (HistoricNewEngland.org); 83 Eric Mailaender's apartment in New York, designed by Resistance Design; 84 designed by Terry Hunziker; 86 left A house in France, decorated by Yves Gastou; 86 right David Carter's house in London; 87 De Stad, Amsterdam, designed by Next Architects; 88 right Emmanuel Renoird's house in Normandy; 88 left Jackye Lanham's home; 89 Vicente Wolf's apartment in New York; 90-91 a house in Virginia designed by Solis Betancourt; 93 above left Vicente Wolf's apartment in New York; 93 above right Agnès Emery's house in Brussels; 93 centre right a house in New York designed by Shelton, Mindel & Associates; 93 below left Hanne Kjaerholm's house in Copenhagen, Denmark; 93 below right designed by Frédéric Méchiche; 94 a home featuring Jane Churchill fabrics; 95 Nicolas Vignot's apartment in Paris; 96 left Fred & Helen Collin's house in London; 96 right James Mohn & Keith Recker's apartment in New York; architecture by James Mohn and interior design as a collaboration between Keith Recker & James Mohn; 97 above left Designed by Pierre d'Avoine Architects; 97 above right Harriet Maxwell Macdonald's apartment in London, designed by Harriet Maxwell Macdonald at Ochre; 98 House in Brooklyn, New York, designed by Ogawa Depardon Architects; 99 Karim Rashid's apartment in New York; 100 left an apartment in London designed by Nigel Greenwood; 100 right Alberdingh Thijmstraat, Amsterdam, designed by Marc Prosman Architecten; 102 above John Barman's apartment in New York; 102 below left James Gager & Richard Ferretti's Pennsylvanian house; 102 below right Mark Badgley and James Mischka's New York apartment; 103 Tricia Foley's house on Long Island; 104 Greville & Sophie Worthington's house in Yorkshire; 105 Robert Kaiser residence. Florida, designed by Gene Leedy; 106 Maureen Paley's house in London; 107 above Baldassare La Rizza's apartment in London; 107 below Frank Faulkner's house in Upstate New York; 109 right the home of Carolyn van Outersterp of CVO in the North East of England; 110 left the home of Carolyn van Outersterp of CVO in the North East of England; 110 right Penthouse loft in New York designed by Bruce Bierman Design Inc.; 111 Harriet Maxwell Macdonald's apartment in London, designed by Harriet Maxwell Macdonald at Ochre; 112 left Robert Kaiser residence. Florida, designed by Gene Leedy; 112 right Martin Harding's house designed by Audrey Matlock; 113 left Mr & Mrs Boucquiau's house in Belgium, designed by Marina Frisenna; 113 right Katy Barker's Paris apartment, designed by Laurent Buttazzoni; 114 above designed by Michael Wolfson; 114 below left Lincoln/Orum residence, Suffolk. Interior by Angi Lincoln; 114 below right Dominique Picquier's house in Paris; 115 Reed & Delphine Krakoff's Manhattan townhouse, designed by Delphine Krakoff of Pamplemousse Design Inc.; 116 above Walter Gropius House, a property of Historic New England (HistoricNewEngland.org); 116 below Greville & Sophie Worthington's house in Yorkshire; 117 Dominique Kieffer's house in Paris; 118-119 Bob & Pam Levin's house in Bel Air, designed by Lynn von Kersting; 120 above Sera Hersham Loftus' house in London; 120 below Dominique Picquier's house in Paris; 121 an apartment in London designed by Nigel Greenwood; 122-123 Nathalie Lété's house in Paris; 123 Sera Hersham Loftus' house in London; 124 Weaving/Thomasson residence, London; 125 above a house in Delhi, designed by Abraham & Thakore; 125 below designer, Nathalie Hambro's apartment in London; 126 Dominique Picquier's house in Paris; 127 left designed by Stephen Sills and James Huniford; 127 right Alex van de Walle's apartment in Brussels; 128 left Vicente Wolf's apartment in New York; 128 right Hunt Slonem's apartment in New York; 129 Reed Krakoff's apartment in New York, designed in collaboration with Pamplemousse Design; 130 Hunt Slonem's apartment in New York; 131 Ann Mollo's house in London; 132 Colette's restaurant at The Grove, Hertfordshire, designed by Fox Linton Associates; 133 Glen Senk and Keith Johnson's house in Philadelphia; 134 Jamie Drake's East Hampton Home; 135 left Malcolm Carefree & Denise Figlar; 135 right Charles de Selliers' house in Brussels.

Acknowledgements

It has been a delight to write a book devoted to the vintage home — a fun, thrifty and deeply topical style, perfect for today. So thank you, Jacqui and Jo, for asking me to write it! Many thanks to Hilary for spectacular editing, to Ash and Nadine, for an inspiring layout and pictures, and to Lesley, for smooth-running support. Thank you Anthony, Cicely and Felix, for your unwavering encouragement. And thanks to my parents, Harry and Ann, who taught me never to throw away, but to rescue, renew and enjoy precious treasures from the past.